A
New View
of an
Old Horizon

A
New View
of an
Old Horizon

Dena M. Bedsole

For more information: dmbedsole@bellsouth.net

Cover photo courtesy of Jen Cowsar Photography
www.jencowsar.com

Photo (opposite) by Amanda Helms

Book design by:
Arbor Books, Inc.
www.arborbooks.com
Printed in the United States of America

A New View of an Old Horizon
Dena M. Bedsole

1. Title 2. Author 3. Memoir

Library of Congress Control Number: 2013901459
ISBN: 978-0-615-75979-1

To my father, "Crazy Eddie," and the legacy he left behind.
May your example lead others to Christ's love
and to the gift of eternal life.

TABLE OF CONTENTS

CHAPTER I

Blessed Beginnings

"Wherever your treasure is, there your heart and thoughts will also be."
    —Matthew 6:21 (New Living Translation Bible)

When I first learned that my father had been diagnosed with pancreatic cancer, writing this book couldn't have been further from my mind. In fact I didn't think about much of anything on that awful July morning in 2010; the only thing that penetrated that haze of shock and fear was the knowledge that my life would never be the same again. It was over the next year, as I watched my father's slow, agonizing death and the disintegration of my family as I knew it, that I first began thinking about what I could do to help others facing the same fate. I also wanted to pay tribute to Eddie Dixon, my earthly father, as well as my Heavenly Father for all the miracles they have brought into my life.

This tragic story stands out in stark relief from an otherwise blessed life. At thirty-three years old, I had my wonderful husband Russell, two beautiful children, and a fulfilling career as a certified registered nurse anesthetist (CRNA). I also had all the usual responsibilities associated with adulthood: balancing family, career, and friends; managing finances and maintaining a household. But this, I soon learned, was all just a dress rehearsal for what was to come. For up until this point, I was still very much my father's little girl.

Dad had always been my pillar of strength, my go-to person in both good times and bad, and that guiding voice inside my head when I had to make a tough decision. He was also my biggest fan and the family peacekeeper. But the biggest role Dad played in my life (and the one I miss the most) was that of trusted counselor. When I was in college, his daily e-mails alleviated my chronic homesickness. Whether it was a long note about how proud he was of me or just a one-line joke, the message was always uplifting and encouraging. Even after I got married and had children of my own, he was still a huge influence in my life.

I had come to depend on these things like they were air and food, but all that changed forever when he became sick. As the battle for my father's life began, my world was thrown into turmoil on every level and in ways I could not have anticipated. I became both child and parent—utterly helpless yet completely empowered, a medical authority and a skeptic of science. From one moment to the next, I vacillated from stony certainty that I was doing the right thing to feeling like I was an impotent fool, making all the wrong decisions that would only further damage my family.

As odd as it may sound, the idea to write this book first came to me in the depths of these wretched times. These were the moments when I was putting on a brave face for everyone else, even though I felt like I was dying inside. At the end of each impossibly long day, I would put the kids to bed and kiss my husband good night, then seek out a moment of solitude and completely break down. I was so exhausted that I had no idea where I would find the strength to do it all again the next day. It was then that I knew I would write this book to let other people who are suddenly thrust into the caretaker role know they're not alone.

At the time I wrote this, I was still very much in a state of flux. That is to say, it was still a daily struggle first to accept the fact that my dad was gone and second to find a way to fill the gaping hole in my heart. In the days immediately following his death, I walked around in a strange, numb state. I felt almost disconnected from my body, and at work I found myself forgetting things that a CRNA has no business forgetting. As the first anniversary of his passing approached, my daily life resumed some sense of normalcy. But that did not mean that the pain had subsided; it only meant that the process of dealing with it had become more internal.

I continue to grieve, not only for my mother and myself but also for my children, who will grow up without their beloved Paw Paw. My son Brooks was only three when Dad died, but they had already formed an incredible bond. My daughter Willa, who was an infant at the time, will know him only through photos and anecdotes. The best I can do is to remind them of what kind of man their grandfather was and to pass along the many valuable lessons he taught me.

Without a doubt, the most difficult emotion to process is the guilt. I understand—both as a rational adult and a medical professional—that I could not have saved my father; I also know I was a loving daughter to him both before and during his illness. In the darkest moments of my grief, however, rational thought goes out the window. That's when I remember things like the family cruise we took when I was thirteen weeks pregnant with my first child.

We were all excited about the trip but no one more so than Dad. One day all of us—Mom and Dad, Aunt Sandi and Uncle Lamar, and Russell and I—got off the ship for an excursion into a small town in Mexico. Dad was never much of a drinker, but he did love banana daiquiris, and that day he loved them a little too much. I was so mortified by his happy yet exceedingly loud behavior that I refused to speak to him the rest of the day—even as we boarded the bus that would take us back to the ship. When I look back on that day now, I realize what a fool I was and how much I took for granted, because I miss those "embarrassing" moments just as much as I miss all the other moments with him.

Then there were the many times during Dad's illness when I felt horribly guilty for all my shortcomings, both real and imagined. I felt guilty when I wasn't able to be with my parents because of obligations at home or work; I also felt guilty for not spending enough time with Russell and the kids. During that year I wore many hats: medical consultant, liaison with Dad's doctors, and companion to my mother to name a few. Exhausted and overwhelmed, I often felt that I was underappreciated, and then I felt guilty for that feeling.

I am still in the process of dealing with these raging emotions. And though I understand that these emotions are common to every person (especially those grieving a loved one), they are still incredibly painful. Sadness, loneliness, and the sense of being a ship without a rudder: these have all become my daily companions.

Given all that I have just said, you may be wondering

why I wrote this book when my father's passing was still so raw. My answer is that this is *precisely* why I wrote it at this time. Most so-called self-help books are written at a comfortable distance from a traumatic event or condition, presumably after the author has had time to process the event and is able to offer some sort of objective advice. You may, if you've read some of these books, even think that I am a little strange to have written it at this time or that I am doing so simply as a vehicle for my own catharsis. I have often thought this as well, but while it is true that writing this book has been extremely healing for me, it is not my primary purpose. I wrote this book from the perspective of helping others who are watching someone they love battle cancer. This is what I wished for when my father was sick, and if I can provide comfort for even one person, my mission will be fulfilled.

A key piece of this mission is to let people know that I would never have made it through this experience without God's love and guidance. I was already a practicing Christian when my father was diagnosed; that is to say, I believed in God and regularly attended church. I even realized, as I will talk about later, that He was preparing me for a storm in my life. But looking back at that time, I can see that my relationship with Christ was superficial and perhaps even a bit hypocritical.

For example when I found out that my dad was sick, I

didn't think about God at all. I remember thinking only that I had to call Russell. The prayers came later, urgently whispered and born of desperation. I prayed often and for very specific things, like *please carry him through the surgery, please increase his appetite, please ease his nausea and vomiting, please help me to explain what is going on to my sweet children,* and *please carry me through my job and my sudden loss of day care.* (My parents watched my children while Russell and I were at work.) Notice that I am not saying that I went to Scripture for guidance; at this point I was still trying to handle things on my own. Still God answered my every prayer.

Through Him my family and I were showered with an incredible amount of love, prayers, and support. Meals and money were provided for us at the hospital. Friends also brought food to our home so that Russell and the kids would have something to eat while I was with my parents at the hospital. We received more cards, letters, and e-mails than we could ever hope to respond to, but the kind words meant the world to us.

I now know that during this time God was slowly changing my heart, often in the most pragmatic ways. My dad had chemo each Monday, and thanks to my wonderful coworkers, I was able switch to the Sunday night shift so that I could be there for his treatments. Sunday evenings are fairly quiet at the hospital, so there was plenty of downtime.

I would slip into the private call room and sit down to read my Bible. On those evenings it was the first time, outside of church, that I had time to really take in my dad's situation. The Bible can be intimidating, and at first I didn't even know where to start. But God has a way of showing you what you need to know. Toward the end of Dad's life, I realized that I was continuously talking to God, sometimes thanking Him, sometimes bargaining or begging Him, but those daily conversations changed the course of my spiritual life forever.

God showed Himself to me at many points in this awful journey. Sometimes I was blessed enough to recognize it in the moment. For example I was always grateful for the fact that I am in the medical profession with its many advantages. The moment I learned that Dad was sick, I ran to our general surgeon and asked, "What do I do? Where do I take him?" Even in my panic, I knew how fortunate we were to have immediate access to doctors who would give us honest answers. I was also part of the small, tight-knit anesthesia community. This meant that Dad had handpicked nurses, nurse anesthetists, anesthesiologists, surgeons, and oncologists. This was such an unbelievable gift, and my heart goes out to anyone dealing with a serious illness without that kind of network.

Another saving grace was the fact that my father was

able to spend much more time at home. Most people with pancreatic cancer (and many types of cancers, for that matter) would have had to go back and forth on a daily basis for treatments or even be admitted for long periods of time. Instead my mother (who is also a nurse) and I were able to give him his medications at home. We even started IVs on him when he was very sick and dehydrated from the chemo.

The existence of other small miracles have dawned on me in a series of aha moments since my dad's passing. I am only now beginning to see the intricate pattern of God's plan and to realize that He had been preparing me for this storm throughout my entire life. This awareness, while often still blurred by pain, continues to help me recover from my father's death and gives me reassurance that I will not only find acceptance but joy. Although you may not realize it now, God has also prepared you for the storm you are facing, and like me He will take you through it and heal you in its aftermath. This is true for everyone, regardless of where he or she is spiritually. You begin your relationship with the Lord where you are at the moment, but God has always been there.

It is no accident, for example, that I am a nurse. I chose the profession for what now seems like the most ridiculous reason: my boyfriend at the time lived back in my home-town, and the associate's degree nursing program was the fastest way for me to get back to him. I have often laughed at the immaturity of my eighteen-year-old self, and at the irony that, while the guy is long gone, nursing is still a huge part of my life. But I never realized until my father was diagnosed that my "silly" decision had been guided by God. This was one of many ways that He had prepared me for what was to come. As a nurse I knew what to expect when my dad was sick, and sadly I also knew what the probable outcome would be. God had also empowered me with the knowledge and skills to comfort my parents and assist in my father's treatment.

Of course knowing that God is there does not mean that you won't feel alone, lost, and scared. In these moments I still turn to the Bible for its immeasurable wisdom and comfort. That's why I have begun each chapter of this book with Scripture that I feel captures where I was at that point in the story. These passages are for you to meditate on and to guide you as you go through the chapters. Whether you regularly read the Bible or not is irrelevant. Simply think of them as food for thought. How does this particular line of Scripture relate to your own situation? How can it help you through this phase of your loved one's illness? What feelings does it bring up for you?

Cancer is many things, but if I had to sum it up in one word, I would say that it is a thief. It steals not only lives but the joy of living. It steals not only your relationship with the loved one who is sick but with everyone you care about: from the friend you don't have time to meet for lunch anymore to your own children, who are too young to understand why they haven't seen you for days on end. What I am hoping you will learn from my story is that even while cancer is stealing everything from you, God is there to show you the way. The most important thing to remember is that you are never alone.

CHAPTER II

Planting Seeds

"Jesus asked, 'How can I describe the Kingdom of God? What story should I use to illustrate it? It is like a tiny mustard seed. Though this is one of the smallest of seeds, it grows to become one of the largest plants, with long branches where birds can come and find shelter.'"
—Mark 4:30-32 (New Living Translation Bible)

I did not grow up in a particularly devout household, which is to say my parents believed in God but didn't regularly attend church; mostly we went on major holidays like Easter and Christmas. God was powerful but removed— an abstract entity that I was taught to pray to for things I wanted but not necessarily to speak to on a daily basis. I certainly wasn't versed in Scripture; I only knew what I heard in church. It wasn't until I went away to college and a friend gave me a Bible that I had any interest in it at all. It would be many more years before God would become a daily part of my life, but I can still remember the day that first seed was planted.

Throughout my father's battle with pancreatic cancer, I often found myself thinking back over my childhood, particularly my father's role in it. Since my father's passing, however, thoughts of my relationship with him have, for some reason, led me to thoughts of my relationship with God as my Heavenly Father. Maybe this was because it seemed that just as one moved out of my life, the other was taking a stronger hold. I cannot help but realize that the loving support and guidance Dad gave me prepared me not only for marriage, motherhood, and my professional life but for my role during his illness. It has also allowed me to see that God, too, had been planting the seeds that would give me the strength to deal with our family's loss.

We may not have been a religious family, but we were certainly a happy one. And at its core was the strong bond between my parents Eddie and Edna. Their relationship was filled with a deep respect, as well as a certain lightheartedness, and I learned at a very young age that a healthy sense of humor is critical for many things in life—and none more critical than a successful marriage. From the first night they met, my dad's quirky inner comedian—referred to as Crazy Eddie by his friends—was a third party in their relationship.

When my dad's best friend David invited him to go the Chattahoochee County Fair, he immediately accepted. For more than a century, the fair had been a Georgia institution, and back in 1969 it was still one of the most important social events of the year. Every autumn folks came from all over the state to take in the midway rides, pig races, live music, and traditional Southern food. Joanne, my dad's girlfriend at the time, couldn't make it, but that was okay; it was a chance for him to spend time with David and his wife Maureen. When he pulled up to the house that night in his shiny 1957 Ford, he had no idea that his life was about to change forever.

My mother Edna Mae Windham didn't say yes right away when her friend Maureen called to ask her to go. Sure she loved the fair, but she didn't want to be a third wheel.

"That's nonsense," Maureen said. "Besides David's friend Eddie is coming, too."

Edna finally agreed.

At first she didn't take much notice of David's friend. She was just looking forward to having a good time at the fair, and besides she too was dating someone else: a perfectly nice guy named Joe. Edna and Eddie didn't speak much as the four of them squeezed their way through the crowded fairgrounds. Edna was catching up with Maureen, while David and Eddie traded good-natured barbs, just as they had done since they were young. They stopped to listen to one of the bands for a while, then stuffed themselves on BBQ pork, corn fritters, and pecan pie before continuing to explore. Eventually they found themselves inside the house of mirrors.

As she walked through the dimly lit hallway, Edna suddenly felt something grab her left breast. Startled, she looked down to see a pale hand reaching through a hole in the wall. Quick as a flash, the hand pulled back, and when Edna bent down to peer into the hole, there was Eddie Dixon's shocked face staring back at her. There was an uncomfortable pause; then they both burst out laughing. To this day when she tells the story of how they met, my mother always adds, "Now that's what you call a boob job!"

As my father told the story, he knew he wanted to marry Edna from the moment they met; it was a true case of love at first sight. For my mother, though, it took a bit longer. About a month later, David and Maureen invited both of them over for Thanksgiving dinner, and it was then that Edna and Eddie finally realized that they were pawns in their friends' cleverly devised matchmaking operation.

Afterward they took a drive up to Pine Mountain, a beautiful area at the foot of the Appalachians. They got out of the car and were talking, laughing, and horsing around— that is until Edna sprayed Dr Pepper all over Eddie's prized '57 Ford. Despite his love for the car, Eddie handled the incident with good humor, and from there Edna slowly fell in love with him.

They were married soon after, on September 25, 1970,

and on their wedding night they drove to the Dixons' family cabin on Lake Harding in Alabama. There had been a lot of food at the wedding, but the bride and groom had been too busy with their guests to eat much. Eddie was famished, but when they got there, they found the cabin stocked with nothing but Dr Pepper and a can of tuna fish. Eddie again laughed it off, but never forgot. On their fifteenth anniversary, he took Edna to a lovely, rather formal restaurant. Imagine her surprise when their waiter appeared at the candlelit table, carrying a tray with a can of tuna and a Dr. Pepper! This willingness to greet life's little annoyances with grace and humor was one of the things that made Crazy Eddie such a beloved member of our family.

Sometimes Dad was funny without intending to be. Before I was born, my parents lived in an apartment complex. One night they thought they heard someone trying to get into their truck. My dad jumped up and ran to the front door. When he opened it up, he saw their next-door neighbor standing there, her mouth hanging open in shock. My father slept in the nude back then, and in his haste to catch the car thieves, he had neglected to throw on clothes. The neighbor got an eyeful, and my parents laughed about it for weeks after.

Wherever he went Dad liked to stir things up by creating scandal and gossip. It tickled him, and we loved the enjoyment he got from it. One day when we still lived in

Vidalia, my dad was outside doing yard work. It was a particularly hot day, and as Dad paused to take a sip of ice water, he noticed Mrs. Sotheby driving down the street. She was new to the neighborhood, and when she saw my father standing there, she pulled over and rolled down the window. Thinking she was there to introduce herself, my dad smiled and walked over to the car.

"Hello," she said formally, "I just moved in down the street, and I was wondering how much you charge Mrs. Dixon to do her landscaping."

Dad realized she had mistaken him for a gardener and was not about to miss such a juicy opportunity.

"Nothing," he replied without missing a beat, "I just sleep with her on occasion."

Mrs. Sotheby gasped and sped off. Dad never bothered to tell her the truth—not even when we sold the house and moved to Alabama. We never knew when Crazy Eddie would make an appearance, but when he did, it was always memorable for years to come.

My father wore many other hats in the family as well, including those of peacekeeper and role model. But as far back as I can remember, he was also my number one cheerleader. When I was a small child, he climbed up on the stage of my first dance recital to hand me a bouquet of pink silk flowers and kiss my cheek. When I graduated from college, the crowd was asked to hold their applause until all the names had been called. But that didn't matter to my father. As I walked across the stage to receive my diploma, I heard a voice bellow, "Go, Turnipseed!" Even if I hadn't seen my father waving frantically from the audience, I would have known it was him. He'd called me Turnipseed for as far back as I could remember. Crazy Eddie also made an appearance in 2002 when Brookwood Medical Center honored me with the Nurse of the Year Award. Unbeknownst to me, my dad had taken the day off from work to be there. Imagine my surprise when he once again joined me on the stage, handed me pink roses, and kissed me on the cheek, exactly as he had when I was a little girl. That's how he made me feel all the time: like the prima ballerina, the brightest star, the most valuable player on the field.

Mom and I were close, too, but like so many mothers and daughters, we bickered throughout my teenage years and well into my young adulthood. I always called my dad whenever she made me mad, especially when I thought I was right (which was all the time). I can still see him, walking into the kitchen with the steely determination of a man about to handle negotiations of the utmost delicacy and importance. Then, as elegant as any UN diplomat and just as shrewd, he would broker a truce between us. A lot of fathers might have grown tired of always being the middleman, but Dad never lost his patience with us. All that mattered to him was keeping his girls happy. I often wondered whether he was just telling us both what we wanted to hear, but whatever he did, it always worked, and peace was restored at least until the next time.

He was never what most would call a strict disciplinarian, but he certainly let me know, in his own subtle way, when I had done something wrong. Like most high school students, I lived for Friday nights when my friends and I would hang out at someone's house or at the local McDonald's. I was never a big drinker, but one night I had two beers too many. Even in my inebriated state, I wasn't worried about going home drunk. My mom was working the late shift at the hospital, and Dad never waited up. Until that point, he'd always said he trusted me and acted accordingly.

The house was dark as I staggered up to the front door, pulled out my keys, and slipped inside. Soundlessly I slipped out of my coat and hung it by the door; then I gingerly placed one foot in front of the other to cut through the living room as I had done a thousand times before. I knew the layout by heart, so I was stunned by a sharp pain in my shin as it made contact with something large and unyielding. In no condition to balance myself, I tripped, caught air, and with a loud grunt, landed on something hard.

"What the—?"

Then the room was flooded with light, and I realized I was lying on the coffee table. Across the room my father stood against the wall, his hand still on the light switch. He was wearing his pajamas and a look of disappointment.

I've often wondered what prompted him to test me that night; although since becoming a mother, I've chalked it up to parents' intuition. Whatever the reason, my dad had calmly rearranged the living room furniture; then he sat down in the darkness and waited for me to come home. He didn't say a word, but the look on his face was punishment enough.

Dad was always there not only to celebrate my successes but also to cushion my failures, and he made every one of these moments a chance for me to grow as a person. Cheerleading was a big part of my life in high school, so much so that I felt it almost defined me. On the day of the eleventh-grade tryouts, I held my breath as I listened to them call the names of the chosen. I was concentrating so hard on hearing my name that it took a moment for me to realize that they had not called it. I tried to breathe, but the crushing weight of disappointment made it difficult. Finally I hung my head and began to cry to my mortification. Suddenly I felt a gentle hand on my shoulder. It was Dad, of course; I had almost forgotten he was there. Knowing words were insufficient. He didn't say a word; he just lifted me to my feet and held me until I started to feel better. That day I learned that whether I was a cheerleader or not, I was still important, because I was his daughter.

Later when I went away to college and was having a hard time adjusting to life in the dorms, Dad's e-mails were a daily reminder that no matter how tough things got, support was never far away. Whether it was a long letter about how proud he was of me or just a one-line joke, the message was always uplifting and encouraging.

"Hiya, Sweetheart," he wrote on one particularly challenging day. "Mom and I know what you are going through; however, it will all be worthwhile. Your independence depends on your education. You can and will be your own person."

Other times he sent me funny little notes about what was going on back home.

"Hi, Doodle. Boy, the weather was rough this morning. I am supposed to play in a golf tournament this afternoon, but I'm not sure how I feel about putting from a boat."

And then there was the e-mail I will never forget: "You will be a good nurse and a great person. I would be pleased to have you as my nurse. I really hope this never happens, because if [I] ever get sick enough to need you as a nurse, I'm afraid I might be on my way to the Promised Land."

He meant this as a joke, of course, but it turned out to be an eerie harbinger of things to come.

On my twentieth birthday, he sent me another note that seemed to predict the future. After telling me what a precious gift I had been to both him and my mother, he wrote, "We have watched you grow into a beautiful young woman with all the qualities that we would pray God would give you. Now you will go forward with your life and become what you and God have planned for you. We often forget that all things are created and planned before we are ready for them. That does not mean that we cannot change the future; however, it does mean that our future is planned and that the plan maker is greater than we can imagine."

His notes contained so many lessons about life, friendship, love, and having confidence in one's abilities. They encapsulated all that my parents had instilled in me and were like a reference book I could return to over and over when I was confused or down.

"You are learning about life in real time," he wrote. "Friends are those individuals that are always there for you, regardless of the situation or the circumstances. They are to be trusted but not depended upon, for we all live very independent lives…. Do not expect others to be the way you want them to be. But always be the way you want to be and remember: be true to yourself. Act and react the way you would like for others to act and react toward you. You will come out the better for taking actions that are pleasing to you."

These notes helped, but I did still feel lonely and out of step my freshman year. One day, deciding I'd had enough, I called Dad from the dorm pay phone.

"I have no friends," I sobbed, "and I want to come home."

My father was always telling me how much he and Mom missed me, so I was sure he'd be thrilled. Images of a warm welcome home flashed through my head, complete with hearty meals and cozy evenings spent watching movies, just like we had when I was a kid. Imagine my surprise—and devastation—when he said no! I could not understand why he would not want me to come home or his uncharacteristically curt tone as he told me so. It wasn't until much later, when I had adjusted to college life, that he told me it was one of the hardest things he had ever done in his life. It had broken his heart to tell me I could not come home, but he knew I needed to learn how to take care of myself. He was showing me that people sometimes need to have the fortitude to do what's best for someone they love—even if it hurts them both. I understood Dad's reasoning; however, I didn't fully appreciate the importance of it until the darkest days of his illness when my mother and I had to make some terribly difficult decisions that would ultimately be best for him.

After getting my associate's degree, I returned home, and life resumed to much the same way as it had before. Although we were all busy with work, friends, and the daily business of living, we always made a point to spend time together as a family. Mom was a night shift registered nurse, and when she was working Dad and I would usually watch TV or just sit around, talking about our day. She often had to work on holidays and other special occasions, and I would stand in as Dad's date. Dad loved to dance, and each year he looked forward to the chance to do this at his company's Christmas party. He was always the first one on the floor and the last one off. Mom and I always laughed because his feet never left the ground; they would just slide. At least he had rhythm, though—something I had not inherited. It didn't matter to Dad; he just put his hand on my back and guided me across the floor to make me look better. The only thing he loved more than dancing was a good joke, and whenever we spoke to coworkers who didn't know who I was, he would purposely not introduce me, hoping they'd think he was on a hot date. As always he loved the idea that he was feeding the office gossip mill, so one year, to help him out, I took one of my friends along, too. Dad was on cloud nine as he showed up with a twenty-something girl on each arm.

We always had a great time together, and Dad always treated me as an equal and a friend. At the same time, however, he was also very aware of how important his approval was to me, and he always wielded this power with the utmost consideration, care, and tact. This held true when I began dating Russell.

I was not a fan of blind dates. So when a friend from work wanted to set me up with a nice guy she knew from church, I said no. Later that week another friend—this one from school—also asked me if I would be willing to go on a blind date with a friend of hers. Again my first instinct was to say no, but eventually the curiosity got the better of me. After all what were the odds of two friends—who had never met each other before—trying to set me up in the same week? It wasn't until I had spoken to both of them again that I realized they were trying to set me up with the same guy! That was just too much of a coincidence for me, so I finally agreed to the date. Russell and I began dating, and it wasn't long before I fell deeply in love with him.

My parents seemed to love Russell, too, so I was completely unprepared when one day my father said he had something to talk to me about; it was something serious about Russell. I nodded hesitantly and followed my father to the kitchen table. He waited for me to sit down; then he sat across from me and took my hand.

"Honey," he began, "I know you're crazy about Russell... but you've been dating for nearly two years, and well... are you sure he's as serious about this relationship as you are?"

He was speaking in his most diplomatic and genteel tone, but the thought that he disapproved of who I was dating was devastating to me. I sat quietly listening and then burst into tears. Dad was quick to explain that he liked Russell just fine, and that he was just making sure he and I were on the same page as far as our relationship was concerned. I sighed with relief when I realized that, once again, Dad forced himself to say something difficult because it was in my best interest.

Thankfully it soon became a moot point. Not long after that conversation, Russell proposed to me on the beach, and it was pure magic. The first thing I said was an ecstatic yes. The second was, "Did you talk to my dad?" Smiling, he assured me that he had; for besides being a wonderful guy, Russell also knew the family he was marrying into. He had not, however, spoken to my mom, and she was shocked when I called to tell her that I was engaged. Shocked and more than a little angry that she had been kept in the dark. My dad knew she couldn't keep a secret and didn't want her to ruin the surprise for me.

As I went about the joyful business of planning my wedding, one thing weighed heavily on my mind. My dad had always been the man in my life, but now that was going to change. I was grieving a bit, and I knew he was, too. I tried to think of a way to let him know that nothing would ever change how important he was to me, but I couldn't seem to find the right words. Then God brought the right words to me when I was least expecting it. I was in line at the grocery store, staring absently at the candy, magazines, and trinkets placed there to entice people on their way to the register, when a silver novelty coin caught my eye. I picked it up, smiling as I read the inscription, then placed it in my cart. It was perfect.

On the morning of my wedding, I stood in my parents' kitchen, having a quick cup of coffee before going to my old room to get ready. When my father walked in, I reached into the pocket of my robe, pulled out the coin and handed it to him. His eyes widened in confusion as he took the piece of cheap metal. Then they welled with tears as he read the words: "A father like you is hard to find—who's honest, strong, wise, and kind." He grabbed me in a tight hug, and I knew that five-dollar coin was the best money I'd ever spent. Dad left it on the table where it was later spotted by my maternal grandmother. Granny had grown up very poor, and bless her heart, she pocketed my dad's coin, thinking it was a quarter! She eventually realized her mistake and returned it to its rightful owner.

I think Dad and I both felt a little better after I had given him the coin. Still as he walked me down the aisle toward the new life that awaited me, I felt his arm shake a little. Or was it mine? I couldn't tell. It seemed to take forever to reach the altar, and when the preacher asked who was giving me away, I heard the quiver in Dad's voice as he answered, "Her mom and I do." Then he began to cry, and I had to elbow him to get him to stop. Looking back, I wish I had let him have his moment, but at the time like any bride, I just wanted everything to go smoothly. He seemed to cheer up when we got to the reception; like always he couldn't wait to get on the dance floor. But as he spun me around in my wedding gown, his eyes welled up again and he whispered, "I'm scared to let you go, sweetheart." I almost started crying myself, but instead I just assured him that we would always be close, and I meant it.

From the beginning Russell and I were very happy together, and I have no doubt that we were meant to be together. I say this not only because we share two beautiful children and a wonderful life together but also because of how we met in the first place. When we met it just seemed to be one of the many times when I was stumbling through life, only to realize later that God had been guiding me the whole time. I also believe that God brought me to Russell so that Russell could bring me back to Him. When we met, Russell was much more spiritually developed than I was. He regularly attended church and encouraged me to do the same. At first, I must admit, I was less than enthused about it. In fact I distinctly remember being more concerned with what I was wearing than with the sermon. After a while I began to enjoy church, but even then I viewed it more as a time to socialize with the new friends I had made than as a time to be with God. I had no idea at the time that, like everything else in my life, He was bringing these wonderful people into my life for a purpose.

Life was good—even better than I had hoped it could be. Russell and I were blessed with two healthy and beautiful children Brooks and Willa. Our professional lives were satisfying as well. Russell loved his work as a deputy sheriff, and like Dad had predicted in all those e-mails he'd sent me during college, my career had blossomed beyond my expectations. After getting my associate's degree from the University of West Alabama in 1998, I continued my education at Samford University, a small private Christian university near Birmingham. There I got my bachelor of science in nursing in 2001, a master of science in nursing with a focus in education in 2005, and a post-MSN graduate certificate with a focus in anesthesia in 2007. Dad and his friends used to joke about the "alphabet soup" after my name. I often said that Samford ought to name a few bricks after me. But with all joking aside, I had begun to look at nursing as a calling rather than a career of convenience. To this day I love every minute of my time spent in the operating room, and I get much more from my patients than I could ever give them.

My relationship with my parents was also stronger than ever, and Russell and the kids only deepened that bond. Russell was their dream son-in-law, and the kids brought new joy and purpose to their lives. They even watched them several times a week, so we didn't have to rely on strangers for day care.

Mom and Dad were settling into their golden years, looking forward to retirement, and watching their grandchildren grow up. Life was not perfect, of course, but it was pretty darn close.

All that was about to change.

CHAPTER III

Diagnosis

"Dear brothers and sisters, whenever trouble comes your way, let it be an opportunity for joy. For when your faith is tested, your endurance has a chance to grow. So let it grow, for when your endurance is fully developed, you will be strong in character and ready for anything."
—James 1:2-4 (New Living Translation Bible)

You might think I'm crazy for saying this, but I felt like God was preparing me for something—something bad, something I was not going to like at all. I had no idea what it was or even if what I was feeling was real. I just couldn't shake it.

I had been having the feeling for a while—this intermittent sense of heaviness. Sometimes I felt it tugging at the back of my mind; at other times it was a slight pressure between my eyes. I couldn't put a finger on it, and for the longest time, I simply tried to pretend it did not exist. Then on one sunny day in June 2010, I was driving along

Highway 119 when I had the sudden, irrepressible urge to say this out loud to someone. There was only one person I knew who would not think I had completely lost my mind, and that was my dear friend Amanda. I grabbed my cell phone and speed dialed her number, thinking that if she didn't answer, I was going to burst. Thankfully she picked up, and I finally gave voice to the feelings that had been weighing on my heart.

When I had finished speaking, Amanda was silent for a moment; then she said, "Okay. First of all you are not crazy. Let's talk about this." I explained this sense of impending doom I'd been having, and how I had been unsuccessfully trying to convince myself that it was a figment of my imagination. True to form she listened without judgment, and although she had no answers as to what this feeling could be about, I felt a little lighter after telling her about it.

"I'm glad you told me," she said, "but, you know, maybe it's nothing. Maybe you're not right."

Unfortunately I was right, but it would take about a month before I learned the nature of my premonition.

Dad had always been a very healthy, active person. While he loved dancing, he was also an avid golfer and bowler. One of his favorite things to do was putter around in the yard. I can barely remember a Saturday when he was not out there, fixing things, planting things, or raking leaves. There was always something to do, and he took pride in doing it all. But in July he began to feel not quite himself; he was tired and his stomach was bothering him. He had indigestion, heartburn, and abdominal pains that were increasing in severity.

"It's probably his gallbladder," Mom said.

I agreed and, after some preliminary tests, so did his doctor. The best bet, he said, was to have his gallbladder removed. It was a simple procedure, and after a brief period of discomfort, my father would feel better than ever. When Dad was admitted on July 29, our spirits were high. We had no way of knowing this was only the first of many painful procedures and treatments he would endure in the coming year.

As expected Dad came through the surgery with flying colors, and that afternoon I took Brooks and Willa to the hospital so they could see their Paw Paw. As soon as we walked into his room, I knew something was terribly, terribly wrong. Beneath his weak but cheerful smile, my father was the color of a fluorescent yellow highlighter. The surgeon insisted everything was fine, but I knew it wasn't normal to look like that after gallbladder surgery. Dr. Marks, his gastrointestinal specialist, agreed and ordered more tests.

A couple of days later, while working in the operating room, I felt the buzz of my mobile through my scrubs.

Normally I would not answer my phone during a procedure, but when I saw it was my mother, a sinking feeling hit my gut. It had to be about Dad's condition; otherwise she wouldn't have called during my shift. The surgeon I was working with realized I was checking my phone, knew what was going on, and gave me a sympathetic nod.

"Mom?" I whispered shakily.

"Dena, honey," she said, and I wondered why she was whispering, too. "Dr. Marks ordered a CAT scan of your father's abdomen. They think he might have cancer of the bile duct."

Instantly I was horrified, but after a few deep breaths, I realized I was relieved as well. The CAT scan—which basically involves an X-ray machine linked to a computer—would take detailed pictures of the organs and blood vessels in Dad's abdomen. Dr. Marks would find the problem; then Dad could begin treatment and start to get well. He would soon be back in the yard, doing what he loved most.

But this was not meant to be. On August 1, I was once again in surgery when my cell phone started vibrating. I remember the feeling of déjà vu as I reached into the pocket of my scrubs and saw it was my mother calling me. A strange foreboding filled me as I took the call, but nothing could have prepared me for the devastating news.

To this day I cannot describe the feeling that came

over me as I heard my mother's hysterical voice say the dreaded words: pancreatic cancer. My tongue felt thick, and I couldn't form a thought. I was struck by a mind-numbing, all-consuming terror. I looked helplessly around the room, knowing there was no way I could continue to work.

The unspoken rule in the operating room is that you never leave your patient. If there were a medical Ten Commandments, this would certainly be one of them. But as I hung up the phone that morning, the surgeon took one look at me and knew I had to go. I had worked with Dr. Koslin and Dr. Kahn for years and considered them not only colleagues but personal friends. Even though I hadn't said a word, they could tell that my world had just imploded.

I managed to hold it together while they arranged for Cindi, another nurse anesthetist, to relieve me. As soon as she walked in, I walked out of the room; told Shay, the administrative assistant, that I was leaving; and headed to the break room, where I fell completely to pieces.

How am I ever going to explain this to Brooks? I thought.

Although my son was only two and a half years old, he already thought his Paw Paw hung the moon. I suddenly flashed back to the Christmas before: my dad and Brooks were on the floor, playing with the new toy jeep Brooks had gotten as a gift. They had begun to forge an incredible bond, and I couldn't bear the idea that he would grow up without the grandfather who adored him and could teach him so much. My next thought was that I had to call Russell and Amanda.

"They'll know what to do," I whispered to the empty room.

What I didn't think about was God. It seems odd to me now, but at that time I was not in a spiritual place to turn to Him first. I just stayed in the break room unable to move, sobbing first to my husband then to my best friend. That's where my coworkers and friends, Cissy and Trish, found me. They sandwiched me in a hug and cried right along with me. As medical professionals we all knew what a diagnosis of pancreatic cancer meant. Despite the decades of fundraisers, research, and advances, it was still ultimately a death sentence.

When I had finally calmed down enough to drive, I left the hospital and headed for my parents' house, where we discussed the next steps. I was horrified when my mother asked me to call my aunt Sandi, Dad's sister, to tell her about the diagnosis. As I picked up the phone and dialed her number, it seemed like the hardest thing I would ever have to do. Now looking back it was just one of hundreds of unfathomably horrible things I would have to do over the next twelve months. Sandi lives in Fortson, Georgia, but as soon as she heard she jumped in the car and drove to Alabama.

The next few days were a terrifying blur. Mom, Dad, and I met with Dr. Heslin, the oncology surgeon, to learn about our options. After Dad was diagnosed, I had done some research on pancreatic cancer, so I wasn't surprised when Dr. Heslin said he believed that the Whipple procedure would be Dad's best bet. He pulled out a pen and a piece of paper and began moving his hand quickly across the page. When he was finished, I saw that he had sketched a rudimentary diagram of the abdominal organs. My eyes went straight to the tadpole-shaped organ in the middle of the page. It was the pancreas, a six-inch organ that sits between the stomach and the backbone.

Even as I stared at the drawing, I felt like I was floating above the room, watching the whole thing happen to some other family. It all seemed incredibly surreal. Not two months earlier, my seemingly healthy dad had traveled back and forth to Florida to help his own father recover from cellulitis in his leg. Dad had tended to my grandfather's home and kept up his garden of peas and butter beans.

"The Whipple is a major surgical procedure," Dr. Heslin said, bringing me back to the present moment.

He pointed to the diagram with his pen.

"It involves not only the head of the pancreas but the bile duct, several lymph nodes, and other abdominal organs."

The Whipple was not an option, he said, when there had already been any metastasis—or spreading—of the cancer.

Dr. Heslin told us he had seen a suspicious spot on Dad's inferior vena cava, which is a large vein that carries blood from the lower abdomen to the heart. This area is sometimes affected by pancreatic cancer, but since Dr. Heslin could not be sure the spot was malignant, he agreed to go ahead with the Whipple. Dr. Heslin scheduled the procedure for August 10—less than two weeks after my father had had his gallbladder removed and less than two weeks since my family's entire world had been shattered.

Determined to stay busy, I took up the task of informing our large circle of friends and family. First I called everyone to tell them about the diagnosis, then I set up a Caring Bridge journal—an online site where people could get updates on my father's condition. Most importantly I asked people to pray for him as he went through treatment. I promised to post regular updates about his progress—that is until Dad would be able to do it on his own.

With his characteristic faith and fortitude, Dad said as he prepared himself for the surgery, "God has control, and I'm a passenger in his recovery vessel." As they wheeled him away to the operating room, Mom, Aunt Sandi, my grandfather, my brother Mike, and I sat down and braced ourselves for the agonizing wait ahead. Four and a half hours later, Dr. Heslin came out and told us the surgery was a success. He believed that he had been able to completely remove the tumor from Dad's pancreas. He still wasn't sure whether the spot on the inferior vena cava was cancer, but either way it had been removed. Now all that remained was to receive the pathology reports. Dr. Heslin told us he was cautiously optimistic about the results.

As I mentioned earlier, because Mom and I were nurses, Dad had the best medical team available. His intensive care unit nurses were incredibly attentive and sweet, perhaps even a little too sweet. They let us see Dad, I believe, a little too soon after he came out of the recovery room. I thought everything I'd read about the Whipple had prepared me for his condition, but I was woefully mistaken. When we walked into his room for the first time, my heart broke into a thousand pieces. He was in so much pain, and there was nothing we could do. I just stood there, my hand in his, telling him to squeeze back when the pain became too much to bear. With the little bit of strength he had, he whispered, "I'm so scared I'm hurting your hand." I had never seen my father like that, and I was instantly struck with the realization that we had absolutely no control over his illness. In my desperation I began silently praying for his relief.

God heard my prayers, and within an hour Dad's condition rapidly improved. He was much more comfortable, and the next time we walked into the room he looked over at us, smiled, and said, "Boy, am I happy to see all of you!"

Mercifully it was as if he didn't even remember our previous visit when he had been groaning with agony, and we all nearly wept with relief. The same day Dad was joking and bonding with his wonderful nurses, and I had the pleasure of updating his online journal to tell everyone the good news.

Dad continued to do well over the next few days. Within two days of his surgery, the nurses were getting him out of bed for walks down the hall. He was allowed to take showers and spend a couple of hours in his chair instead of the bed. They also began his tube feedings, which he tolerated rather well. But the best medicine was his daily conversations with Brooks. I know my son's phone calls to wish him "night, night" did my father far more good than any treatment the hospital could offer.

Three days after surgery, Dr. Heslin came in to deliver the final pathology reports.

"They basically confirmed what we already knew," he said, his eyes full of sympathy, and I wondered how many times he'd had to deliver such devastating news. "Eddie definitely has pancreatic cancer."

My stomach dropped, and I found myself fighting for control. A small part of me had been clinging to the hope that somehow this was all just a horrible mistake. Now my hope was gone and replaced by another dose of paralyzing terror. The doctor offered a weak smile.

"The good news is that nine of the eleven lymph nodes tested were negative," he said.

I felt my family staring at me, waiting for clarification, and I told them it meant Dad had a fighting chance. My father sighed and my mother whispered, "Thank God," but I felt sick. My words were at odds with everything I had ever heard about this disease.

"He'll need chemotherapy," Dr. Heslin said, "and radiation. But we're going to hold off on any treatments until he's fully recovered from surgery and his feeding tube has been removed."

Dad remained in the hospital for a week after his surgery. Mom wouldn't leave his side. She spent every night with him, and it quickly began to wear on her. I was still working my regular three twelve-hour shifts a week, but it was very difficult for me to stay focused. I couldn't bear to be away from my father or my mother for very long. I wanted to be there to take care of them the way they had always cared for me. I spent as much time as I could at the hospital, often heading there straight after my shift. Whenever possible I brought Brooks and Willa with me, and we all spent a lot of time looking at family photos and remembering happier times.

Despite our newfound hope for his recovery, it was still so hard to watch my father struggle to get well. Like most people who have had a Whipple procedure done, he was very sore and often felt nauseated. It only got worse when the doctors removed his nasal feeding tube. He could not be discharged, they told us, until they were sure he could maintain his weight on his own. In the days that followed, every bite of food he kept down was a cause for celebration. Finally the day came when the doctors announced that he would be going home the next day.

As strange as this may sound, I had mixed feelings about this. On the one hand, I was overjoyed that my father would continue his recovery in the comfort of his own home. It would also lessen his chances of contracting one of the potentially deadly infections that run rampant in medical facilities. My mother also desperately needed to get out of there, and I was thrilled she'd finally be able to sleep in her own bed. On the other hand, the Whipple is known for not only a difficult recovery but also a lengthy one. Many patients are utterly exhausted for around three months, and I worried how Dad would do without the team of doctors, nurses, and technicians who had been seeing after his every need. I prayed that his transition would be as smooth and as painless as possible and that God would give me the strength to pick up some of the slack. I also posted on Dad's online care journal, asking his scores of friends to do the same.

Throughout August my dad slowly continued to heal.

Every day was a battle hard won to keep up not only his physical strength but his spirits as well. One thing that gave him great pleasure was updating his care journal on his own. Over the Internet, he could pretend everything was fine. He could act like the same old Crazy Eddie he'd always been, so no matter how he was feeling, he tried to infuse each post with the gumption and humor he was so well known for.

"Good morning, everyone," he wrote on August 23, nearly two weeks after his operation. "Broke loose from the sheets this morning; feeling the best I've felt in quite a while. A good night's rest next to my lady has healing powers all their own."

He wrote about the fantastic meal my mother had made for him that Sunday. Then, so typical of my dad, he took the focus from himself and sent blessings to others.

"I pray for each and every one of you, as you have and are praying for me. Please remember those folks serving our country and preserving our freedom."

The hardest part for him at this time was lying around and doing nothing. It was August, and normally he'd be outside, gardening in the thick summer air. Instead he was trapped inside, willing his body to heal and his mind to remain positive. Still he tried to be upbeat in his updates to his friends.

"I did start my truck and car and let them run until the temperature gauges moved to normal. Listened to CDs in the car for about ten minutes. Sounds too simple to be true, but it is still an accomplishment."

I knew my dad better than anyone, and it broke my heart to hear the helplessness behind the words.

All in all though, this was a time—albeit a brief one—of relief, optimism, and gratitude. I have since referred to it as the calm before the storm—the storm being the chemotherapy and the radiation that was soon to come. In early September Mom, Dad, and I returned to Dr. Heslin's office for Dad's first postoperation visit. The doctor was impressed with his weight, given the loss of appetite many patients experience after a Whipple. My mother had been watching him like a hawk to make sure he ate enough, and her efforts paid off.

The doctor also removed his staples as well as a drain from the surgical site. The removal of the drain was agonizing for him, and he squeezed my hand so hard I thought he would crush it. I bit my lip, trying to imagine how much he was hurting, but I failed miserably. It took all my strength to look into his eyes and see the pain there, but I did, silently willing him to hang on just a little bit longer.

The ordeal took less than thirty minutes, but it seemed to go on for hours. After it was over, Dr. Heslin told us that although he had indeed removed all the cancer, Dad would still need a combination of radiation and chemotherapy. As I absorbed the news, I kept my eyes averted, knowing if I looked at either of my parents I would start crying. Dad had been through so much already, and the fight hadn't even begun. Through the corner of my eye I could see him nodding, too weak with exhaustion to do anything else.

The doctor then spent a few minutes explaining what my father could expect in the coming months, including the painful side effects of both the chemo and radiation. The course of treatment, he added, is a personal choice; some people opt not to undergo it at all. We made it clear to Dr. Heslin that we were in this for the long haul. As we stood to leave, my parents thanked him for all that he had done and for the fighting chance the treatment would give my father. Suddenly I asked the question that had been burning in my gut for weeks: "How long does he have, doctor?" It killed me to ask, but I couldn't bear the thought that my parents were going into this unprepared.

Dr. Heslin's eyes met mine, and I knew he was looking at me not as the daughter of a patient but as another medical professional.

"Eighteen to twenty-four months," he said quietly.

I nodded but didn't say anything else. It was out there, I thought, and that was enough. On the way home, my parents remained optimistic, and I soon realized why. They thought the doctor had meant eighteen to twenty-four months if Dad elected not to have any treatment. But I knew Dr. Heslin was saying something else entirely. In a way though, it didn't matter, because we were all going to fight this with everything we had. I reminded myself that as bad as the prognosis was, it could have been worse, and I thanked God for bringing my father this far.

The next step was a PET scan, so they could get a read on Dad's hypermetabolic activity in the surgical bed, which is just a fancy way of saying his baseline health for starting the treatment. The scan showed a small mass on his lung, but since the doctors were not sure whether it was cancerous or not, they decided to proceed with the scheduled treatment plan. Dad would receive chemo once a week for two weeks; then he'd have a week off, followed by another two weeks of treatments. The radiation schedule would be much more stringent: thirty minutes a day Monday through Friday for six weeks.

The chemo was scheduled for Monday mornings, so I set about rearranging my life so I could be at those sessions. I usually worked on Mondays, but thanks to my fellow CRNAs, I was able to switch to the Sunday night shift instead. My new schedule also meant there would be one less day I'd have to worry about child care. My mom and dad would no longer be able to watch the kids when Russell and I were working, and although I felt terribly guilty for having to think about this, I couldn't ignore reality. I needed to work, and we also needed someone to take care of Brooks and Willa.

This began a new family tradition my kids came to know as their mother's day out. Each Sunday I would work my usual overnight shift; then I'd run home, shower, take Brooks and Willa to school, and finally meet my parents at the hospital. I was exhausted, of course, but the thought of my mother sitting alone there gave me the energy I needed to keep moving. We would wait at the hospital for awhile until we knew my father was settled; then I would take her to lunch. By the time we got back, Dad would be finished and ready to go home. As usual God worked out the timing perfectly for us. I could only continue to pray that He would give us the strength to face the days ahead.

CHAPTER IV

Cancer Won Today

"Don't worry about anything; instead, pray about everything. Tell God what you need and thank Him for all He has done. If you do this, you will experience God's peace, which is far more wonderful than the human mind can understand. His peace will guard your hearts and minds as you live in Christ Jesus."
—*Philippians 4:6-7 (New Living Translation Bible)*

Pancreatic cancer, with its ninety-five percent fatality rate, is considered by most experts to be the deadliest of all cancers. Perhaps the strongest proof of its lethality is that it claims the lives of those with the financial resources to access every treatment known to man, including the very costly experimental drugs on the cutting edge of science. Within the past five years, Luciano Pavorotti, Patrick Swayze, and Steve Jobs all lost their battle with this vicious killer. Despite all the amazing medical advancements we have made in treating other cancers, the survival rates for cancer of the pancreas remain stagnant and dismal. This is largely due to the fact that it is difficult to detect in the early stages.

Treatment is challenging because of the nature and function of the pancreas itself. It is an organ that performs a multitude of functions affecting the body's endocrine and digestive systems. One of these functions is to make pancreatic juices that work with enzymes to break down food. These juices flow through a series of ducts that lead to the lower intestine. The pancreas is also a gland, and it makes insulin and other hormones that travel the body through the bloodstream. This is what makes cancer of the pancreas so likely to spread: the malignant cells are literally transported throughout the body to other organs such as the liver and the lungs. Needless to say it is an extremely debilitating and painful disease.

The goal of surgery is obviously to remove the tumors; the goal of the chemotherapy and the radiation is to hunt and kill any malignant cells left behind. Unfortunately the horror of these treatments rivals that of the cancer itself. Chemotherapy is administered intravenously; the drugs travel through the bloodstream to kill fast-growing cancer cells and hopefully keep the disease from spreading. However, it also kills *healthy* fast-growing cells. It also causes loss of appetite, nausea, vomiting, diarrhea, and mouth sores. Radiation is a completely different process; it involves a large machine that directs high-energy rays at the site of the tumor. The treatment itself is painless, but it also has many brutal side effects, among them nausea, diarrhea, and exhaustion.

These side effects are well known, even to people outside the medical profession, so it was no surprise to any of us that Dad was terribly sick after his chemotherapy. The fact that Mom and I knew what to expect didn't make it any easier to watch him unsteady on his feet and unable to keep down even the smallest meal. Still we thanked God for our blessings. The hospital was only five minutes from their house—close enough that he was able to go home after treatments instead of being admitted like many other patients. It also made a world of difference that Mom and I were able to administer much of the care that most people would have remained in the hospital for. I was beginning to realize even more deeply why God had led me to become a nurse—it allowed me to help my parents through those dark days.

This all became part of my new, brutal routine. After each shift I would work, go over to my parents' house, help Mom take care of Dad, and do anything else she needed me to do around the house. From there I went home to feed Russell and the kids as well as take care of my own household. One day I was preparing a tray of food for my father. He was sitting in the living room, apart from the sound of the TV. Otherwise the house was quiet. A few minutes before, I had sent my mother to bed for a much-needed nap. She had argued with me about it, but she was exhausted, and it was a half-hearted attempt. I looked down at my father's lunch, wondering if he would actually eat any of it when suddenly it hit me: the roles in my family had completely reversed. I was now the primary caregiver—not just to my dad but to both of my parents. I was stepping into my father's shoes. I began to realize that everything and everyone in my life had prepared me for this role, including, of course, my father himself. All the lessons he had taught me as a child, all those e-mails he had sent me in college, were now the core of strength from which I drew, minute by minute, to help them through his illness.

I placed the tray on the snack table in front of my father and kept him company while he forced down a few bites. Then, remembering the pile of laundry collecting in the hamper, I picked up the phone to call my husband and tell him that once again I would not be home in time to make dinner. He was his usual understanding self, of course, and for the thousandth time I thanked God for blessing me with such a wonderful partner. Between my job and the children, there was no way I could have helped my parents if it hadn't been for Russell's endless love and support. More often than not that fall, he worked all day only to come home and play the role of both mother and father to our children. It was like God was continually showing me that I had indeed married the perfect man. Still there were many nights I came home, exhausted, broken-hearted, and angry that my family, which had always been so blessed, was now being ravaged by cancer. I had always heard and believed that God had a plan, but I could not find the rhyme or reason in any of this. My father had brought nothing but joy and laughter to every life he touched, and seeing him in such a weakened state filled me with rage.

It helped that so many people were praying for our family, and I continued to update the online journal whenever Dad was too weak to do it. I ended each post by asking them to send their prayers. My fellow church congregants, who had once been acquaintances I thought about only at Sunday service, became a precious support system as strong as steel.

In October 2010, Dad started receiving radiation in addition to the chemo, and the combination took an awful toll on his body. The nausea and the vomiting continued to grow worse, and he was often unable to eat anything. As bad as it seemed, though, the doctors said he was making progress, and my mom even went back to work one day a week. It did her a world of good to get out of the house and concentrate on others, and I made sure I was always around on that day in case Dad needed me.

Eating had become a challenge for him; he often went a week without eating solid food and had to rely on the feeding tube that had been in place since the Whipple procedure. So when he called me one afternoon and told me he had a craving for egg drop soup, I was thrilled. I hurriedly packed up Brooks and Willa and drove to the nearest Chinese take-out restaurant. I had already parked and gotten the kids out of the car when I realized that, although the front door of the restaurant was open, the lights were off. *That's strange*, I thought. When we got inside the harried cook told me that they had a power outage. Sighing I loaded Brooks and Willa back in the car and headed to another take-out place. They, too, had no power. I was nearly in tears when I pulled up to a third place and found the same situation.

"Please," I told the man behind the counter, "I just need an egg drop soup."

"But it will be cold," the man said, looking at me like I was crazy.

I probably looked crazy, too—wide eyed and frazzled, acting like my life depended on procuring a bowl of soup. After I assured him that I had a microwave, he ladled the precious liquid into a plastic container. I took a deep breath, got the kids back in the car once again, and raced over to my parents' house.

My father's eyes lit up when he saw me and the children; then his eyes went to the brown bag clenched in my hands.

"Is that what I think it is?"

"It sure is," I answered, so happy I was able to give him this one small thing.

I smiled all the way to the kitchen, heated up the soup and served it to my father. I even managed to keep the smile in place when he took two spoonfuls, then sat back in his chair, too nauseous to swallow another bite.

On Monday, November 1, after a rough weekend, Dad went to the cancer center for his regular treatment. As usual he would receive his radiation first, then move down the hall for the chemotherapy. Mom and I stuck around for a while, thinking we would wait until he was getting the chemo before we went to eat. Thank God we did.

I think I felt the nurse rushing toward us before I actually saw her. I looked up from the magazine I was reading and saw her gliding down the white linoleum floor. Suddenly I found it very difficult to breathe. Something was terribly wrong. My mother was sitting next to me, and without a word I gently tapped her on the arm and gestured for her to stand. I didn't trust my voice to speak. It seemed to take the woman forever to reach us, but finally she was standing before us. Unable to speak I simply sat there and waited for her to explain. Dad had seemed okay when he received his radiation, but as the nurse set up his IV for the chemo, everything took a drastic turn for the worse. Dad's heartbeat was dangerously fast, and he was to be admitted to the intensive care unit immediately. Mom and I rushed to the ICU, where a flurry of lab work and other tests had already begun. As awful as he felt, Dad was still aware enough to ask me to update his care journal.

"For any of you," I wrote later that night through a haze of tears and exhaustion, "who are thinking *What can I do?* The answer (and I am so serious) is prayer. Please be in prayer for our entire family and any of Dad's friends who are affected by this. God is our ultimate healer and he hears our prayers."

The next couple of days were much better. The doctors were able to rehydrate him and get his heart back down to a normal rate; he even had some color in his cheeks and managed to eat a little. That was the good news. The bad news came with the test results: Dad had blood clots in both lungs. This is common in pancreatic cancer patients, and Mom and I were actually relieved that the doctors discovered these clots in time to treat them. A procedure was scheduled for the next day to stop any other clots from traveling to his lungs. In the meantime he was allowed to walk the halls a bit, and for this I was thankful. I hated seeing him confined to a bed. As he came back from walking a lap around the ICU, he smiled at me and said, "Happy birthday, Sweetheart." With everything that had gone on in the past forty-eight hours, I had completely forgotten. Those words were the sweetest sound I had ever heard, simply for the fact that Dad felt well enough to remember. I thanked God for this tiny miracle and continued to pray that he would soon have a normal life again.

A week later we celebrated Dad's last radiation treatment. There would be no more daily trips to the hospital. He would now go back to his Monday chemo treatments. That Thanksgiving we had another reason to celebrate: my father was able to eat exactly one bite of his favorite dressing. That one bite made the whole dish worth cooking.

It was around this time that I began to really worry about my dad's mental state. He hadn't really felt good (already a relative term) since August, and he was getting more and more depressed. He was also worried about my mom and the strain his illness was placing on her. I knew very well how important patients' attitudes are to their recovery, but I also knew firsthand how cancer robs people of their lives and how difficult it is to stay positive when they can no longer take part in anything they used to love.

This whole time I was trying to hide my greatest fear: that my father would never be the same again. To cover this fear, I became the cheerleader my father had always been for me. No matter how hopeless I felt, I always made sure I had a smile on my face when I walked through my parents' door. I smiled even more than I had before this whole situation began, but it was window dressing or a piece of jewelry worn only for special occasions. Sometimes I smiled so hard and so long, the grin felt like a tight band around my head.

There were times I even felt underappreciated for all that I was doing. Did anyone even *notice* how much I was doing? How much of my own children's lives I was missing? That I rarely saw my husband, and when I did I was usually either half asleep or in tears? For the most part, they didn't seem to notice, and I resented it. With the small bit of hindsight I have gained since then, I can see I was so busy being strong, so busy not showing my emotions, that those around me didn't realize I was dying inside. Each of us was locked within our own insular world of pain, and no one had anything to give beyond what we gave to Dad. Of course I knew all this, but I am only human, and there were times when I just wanted my sacrifices to be acknowledged. With God's help I have since forgiven myself for feeling this way, but back then the guilt was more than I could bear. On these nights I would wait until the kids were in bed and

Russell had turned in for the night; then I would go into the kitchen, sit down on the floor, and completely fall apart. Sobbing and praying and pleading with God to make my father whole again. I never knew how I was going to get up and do it all again the next day, but somehow God always gave me the strength.

I began to see the hidden blessings in every moment, even when that moment was incredibly painful: the tech's gentle touch when administering the chemo IV, my father's weak but joyous smile when I brought Brooks and Willa to see him, my parents' shared looks of agony that spoke of their forty-year marriage. I watched everything with a heightened awareness I had never experienced before, and each second with my father imprinted itself indelibly on my heart.

That autumn seemed to drag on endlessly; each day's dreadful routine blended into the next. Exhaustion was my constant companion, and I felt like I was walking through life behind a hazy white curtain. Then suddenly it was Christmas. It seemed to come suddenly because every other year had always been an entire season filled with shopping and parties. That year Christmas was just another day, much like any other day in our new normal life. We all tried as best as we could to make it special for my children, but I couldn't help remembering the year before when Dad had joined Brooks on the floor to play with the toy jeep he had gotten my son. The two of them were having a great time, and I knew without a doubt that my son—both of my children—had added years to my father's life. He had certainly behaved like a child that day, crawling around on the floor as he chased Brooks with the jeep, making a gruff *vroom* sound that elicited ecstatic giggles from my son. But by that next Christmas, Dad was a shadow—both physically and spiritually—of his former self.

Somehow though, my parents continued to be optimistic about the fighting chance they believed he had, and on January 7, Dr. Heslin gave them another reason to hope. Dr. Heslin finally felt my father was eating well enough to remove the dreaded feeding tube, which had been embedded in his gut since August 10. This sure sign of progress improved Dad's mood, and he even wrote in his care journal that he had "a big spring planned" and that he hoped his body would allow it.

But as wonderful as this news was, it was nothing compared to the news we received on January 25. Dad had still been on chemo throughout those many months—both with IV chemo and pills given to him at home—and that day was no different. We headed over to the clinic as usual; then we went to see Dr. Ferguson, the oncologist overseeing his treatments, for a regular checkup. When we walked into the office, I immediately noticed the look on the doctor's face. She looked like a woman with a secret—a good secret.

"Well, Eddie," she said, literally beaming. "You have finished your IV chemo. You'll continue the home chemo by mouth for a while, but we're certainly making progress here."

She looked at Dad, at my mother, and finally at me.

"That great, Doc!" my father exclaimed. "I can't say I'm going to miss this place."

My mom and I laughed, and I think it was my first genuine smile in months. Just knowing my father wasn't going to feel as sick and might even be able to enjoy a meal felt like an enormous weight had been lifted from my shoulders. But Dr. Ferguson still had that strange look on her face.

"There's more, Eddie. I just got the results of your most recent round of blood work, and your cancer markers are in the normal range."

These were the words we had longed for since Dr. Heslin told us about the treatment plan, yet the full import didn't sink in right away. Maybe we just didn't dare believe it. We stood there for a moment, dumbly staring at Dr. Ferguson.

"Did you hear what I said?" she asked. "Your cancer markers are normal. Eddie, this means you're in remission!"

Remission. It was the most beautiful word I had ever heard. In a flash Mom and I enveloped my father in a hug, careful not to squeeze too tightly. It was everything we had been praying for so fervently, and I felt like falling to my knees and thanking God right there in the office. Of course then the nurse part of my brain kicked in, and I began asking questions. What did this all mean, really?

The doctor told us that, although there was no indication of cancer in his blood, Dad would still need another PET scan in early March. The scan would detect any recurrence of the tumor in the original site. It would also be able show whether the tumor had spread to his lungs or other organs. He would continue to have blood tests every two to four weeks to make sure those markers stayed within the acceptable range. As Dr. Ferguson had already told us, Dad would take one chemo pill a day from home until the doctors received the results of the PET scan in March. Compared to what Dad had been going through all those previous months, this new plan sounded like a luxury vacation.

Until then, the doctor said, Dad was to concentrate on regaining his strength. He had shrunken to a skeletal 124 pounds, and it was critical that he regain some of the thirty pounds he'd lost since the Whipple procedure. It would be much easier for him to eat once the chemicals were absorbed into his body, and with no more IV chemo treatments, Dad would be able to eat more than he had in six months.

Dad began his next care journal entry with an exuberant,

"Hello Family & Friends: PRAYERS ARE ANSWERED!" After a brief synopsis of our appointment with Dr. Ferguson and the treatment plan moving forward, he thanked everyone for their prayers and support. And he ended with "God has a plan and reason for me being alive. I'm sure He'll show me the light." Dad's words of relief, gratitude, and faith were a moving testament to the power of collective prayer, and I couldn't help but cry as I read them. I had no doubt that the many friends and relatives reading it had the same reaction.

Of course I didn't actually need to read the update. I was there to watch my parents laugh and hug and make plans for a future that just days before had seemed an impossible dream. It was as if, in the eleventh hour, the condemned man had been saved from the hangman's noose. God indeed had a plan, and it was for my father to recover and live the life he was meant to live. He just needed some time to regain his strength; then he'd be fishing in the pond near his house, golfing with his friends, playing with my kids, and enjoying time with my mom. In the days that followed, we all tried to return to some semblance of precancer normalcy. Every moment felt like a precious gift. Yet even as I outwardly rejoiced along with them and even as I wept with gratitude, something in my heart—something small and hard and heavy—was weighing me down like an anchor.

For despite the excellent news we had received, I couldn't quite bring myself to believe it.

Throughout my father's illness, guilt had become my daily companion: guilt that I wasn't doing enough for him, guilt that I wasn't around for Russell and the kids the way I should be, guilt that I felt underappreciated for all I was doing. Now a new guilt had taken up residence in my gut: guilt that I couldn't just be happy my dad was in remission and no longer needed to go to the clinic for IV chemotherapy. After all wasn't this what I had been praying for—what we had *all* been praying for—since he was diagnosed?

At first I tried to convince myself it was my medical training, but no matter what the battery of blood tests and scans showed, I knew pancreatic cancer is tantamount to a death sentence. This reality stared me in the face every time I went to work. All my colleagues at the hospital—even some I didn't work with on a regular basis—made a point of congratulating me on the news, but very few of them were able to meet my eyes. Those who did couldn't hide an unmistakable look of pity. They knew as well as I did that all of us praying for Dad's recovery were probably headed for an enormous disappointment. I could pretend with my parents, my aunt Sandi, and even Russell that my father had beaten the odds, but whenever I had a moment to think, the fear crept back in. As hard as I tried to just have faith, cancer remained an elephant in the room, and it was sitting on my chest. That's where the guilt came in—what kind of Christian was I that my faith in God couldn't overcome the doubt? Even as I was thanking Him for answering our prayers, I couldn't shake the feeling that He was still preparing me for that awful, nameless thing I had told Amanda about all those months before.

I tried to go about my business, making up for lost time with Russell and the kids, caring for my patients, and helping my mother get Dad back to his old self. But soon it became apparent that he was not recovering as quickly as we had hoped. Despite being cancer-free, the weight of the disease still clung to him like a wet blanket. He was physically exhausted and seemed unable to take joy in anything. It was like my sweet dad had gone somewhere else, leaving a sad, angry shell in his place. He spent his days not puttering in the yard but sitting in his recliner, staring off into space. It was as if he had lost all passion for life, and the positive attitude he was known for had been replaced by an icy fear. When I needed to have two surgeries in as many weeks (one for a torn ligament in my ankle), he became irrationally afraid that I would fall with my crutches. I knew this fear was because he felt too weak to help me. Cancer had stolen his confidence in his ability to care for his family, and even the slightest upheaval threw him into a tailspin.

It is common for cancer survivors to feel anger, depression, and extreme fatigue. In fact an estimated twenty-five to forty percent suffer from physical and emotional upheaval in varying degrees, including an emptiness they cannot quite put a finger on. For some these symptoms begin immediately after they finish their treatments. Others experience these symptoms months or even years later.

When people are battling cancer—or any life-threatening disease—they often make promises to themselves, to their loved ones, and to God about all the things they will change if they survive. They might plan to quit the job they hate and follow a long-lost dream. They might make a pact to spend more time with their parents, spouses, kids, friends, or pets. In short they will plan to do everything they put off when they thought they had all the time in the world. After they are told they are either cured or in remission, these people are filled with a new lease on life. Like my dad believed, they also believe they have been spared for a reason, and they will now have the chance to really live. For many people, however, this high seems to fade as daily life takes over. Many people find they cannot just leave their job or they don't have the physical strength to go back to school or to start jogging with the dog each morning. This often leads to feelings of sadness, hopelessness, and even anger. Some people begin to wonder if their survival was really a divine plan or if it was all just a cosmic joke. After all why were they spared if it wasn't because of this chance to dramatically improve their circumstances? Why would God let them live only to see them suffer?

It is also important to remember that the bodies of these cancer patients have quite literally been through hell. Both the diseases and the "cures"—particularly chemotherapy and radiation—have weakened their immune systems and have often caused, as in my father's case, extreme weight loss. These people find themselves trying to recover from the pain they have already suffered as well as the paralyzing fear that this pain could come back again if the cancer returns. We like to believe that we are in control of our lives. Being diagnosed with a life-threatening illness shatters that illusion forever.

For those of us who have never had cancer, it is hard to imagine feeling anything but a joyous new zest for living after the doctor tells us that the cancer is gone; however, research shows that this inability to understand our loved one's experience may actually contribute to the survivor's depression. They often feel misunderstood by those around them as well as guilty and confused that they do not feel happy just to be alive.

I cannot be sure exactly what my father was feeling during those days; we were all trying hard to be upbeat that I don't think anyone asked him if he was depressed. However, I can only guess that the fear and helplessness many cancer patients feel exponentially increases with how lethal the disease is. My dad was well aware of the dismal survival rate for those with pancreatic cancer: it continues to hover around five percent, despite incredible advances in oncology, technology, and other areas of medicine.

I thought about the horrible roller coaster ride my dad had been on since the summer before. Within the space of two weeks, he had been told he had a gallbladder problem, cancer of the bile duct, and finally pancreatic cancer. He'd then undergone the Whipple procedure, chemotherapy, and radiation. On top of that, he had been given a life expectancy of eighteen months. *Eight* months later, the doctors were telling him, "You're cancer-free. Go live your life." No wonder he couldn't process it all! Was he angry at God for letting this happen to him in the first place? Or was he angry at God for healing him without telling him when he would feel better? And what was he supposed to do with the rest of his life? I didn't know, and I couldn't bring myself to mention it to him.

What I did know is that my father no longer enjoyed anything; he hardly ever went outside, even when he felt physically up to it. Instead he chose to spend most of the time in his armchair. Even his visits with his beloved Brooks and Willa weren't the same. Sure he was happy to see them, but the twinkle in his eye was gone, and he certainly wasn't getting on the floor to play with Brooks as he had that last "normal" Christmas. I often found myself wondering whether my children could tell that their Paw Paw had changed. I hoped not. They had already been through so much upheaval in their short lives.

I was also dealing with my own lost expectations about how life would resume once my father was well. Sure I missed dancing with him at the annual Christmas party, but what I longed for the most were the simple, day-to-day things that had always made our relationship special. Before he retired one of my favorite things to do was meet my father and his friend Don for lunch. Whenever he called on my days off, I always answered the phone with a smile, because I knew how the conversation would go. Dad would ask me if I was free around noon, and when I said yes, he'd say, "Great, Sweetheart. Now why don't you meet us here at the office so we can ride together?" And although I'd casually answer, "Good idea, Dad," my smile would grow even wider, because I knew he really just wanted to show me off to his coworkers. After Brooks was born, Dad was so ecstatic to be a grandfather that he insisted I bring the baby along, too. He was proud of the woman I had become and proud of the job he and my mother had done in raising me, and he wanted everyone to know it. It was only one of the many things my father did to make me feel like the most special person in the world; it also reminded me of the kind of parent I wanted to be to my own children. In any event I never refused the offer when he asked me to stop by his workplace.

After catching up for a few minutes with Dad's colleagues, we'd head out to the local Arby's, where Don and Dad had been loyal customers for years. The two of them would sit next to each other on one side of the booth, so they could check out the pretty girls going through the drive-through. Sitting across from them with the huge roast beef sandwich I could never quite finish, I'd just listen to their antics, shake my head, and laugh. Occasionally I even questioned their taste, but I kept my opinions to myself. I knew my dad only had eyes for my mom, so it was all in good fun.

Usually being a regular at a fast food chain doesn't mean much, but Crazy Eddie had an effect on people wherever he went, and Arby's was no exception. Ms. Datcher, the manager, had a special place in her heart for my dad. As soon as she saw his Mustang Shelby pull into the parking lot, she would run to drop the fries into the fryer so they would be extra crispy when he came in. They had become such good friends over the years that she even brought him home-cooked meals on holidays. I never ceased to be amazed by how people reacted to him; he had an uncanny ability to draw them in and charm them with his ever-ready smile and enormous heart.

At the time I remember thinking it was just Dad being Dad; it was only after he had lost his fun-loving spark that I realized how truly blessed I was to have him. He was not only my father, he had also been my mentor, teacher, and best friend when I was growing up. The hardest part of his illness was not being able to talk to him about everything and nothing the way I had before. I missed being able to talk to him in that easy way we had before cancer had crept into our lives. With a chill in my heart, I was beginning to think that we had lost my father on that July day in 2010 when he was diagnosed. I was beginning to think that cancer had stolen my father after all. And that's when I began to wonder what God really had in store for us.

Yet on paper we had every reason to hope for a full recovery. Over the next few months, my dad continued to have excellent test results. In March he had another PET scan, which showed no signs of recurrence, and his blood work in May and June also came back within the normal range. On Tuesday, March 15, my dad posted on the cancer journal about the PET scan results. Again he thanked God for His plan and his friends for their prayers, he then vowed to gain back the rest of the weight he had lost during treatment. All he needed was some rest and some heaping plates of my mother's cooking. Even against my better judgment, I began to believe that the worst was behind us. I tried to beat my inner nurse into submission and concentrate on the positive.

Even as I wrote this book, I couldn't believe how cruel, sneaky, and insidious cancer could be. It tricked us into believing it had left us alone, all the while quietly lurking and laughing as my father went through the tests that told us he was in remission. It was waiting for the one moment we would let our guard down and start planning for the future. Then it hit us even worse than before, knocking us down so hard we felt like we'd never get up again. Cancer steals not only lives but trust in life.

Cancer will also steal your trust in God if you let it. During these months of remission when my father was living this strange half-alive life, I began to question the meaning of answered prayers. We had prayed the cancer away, yet my father had no quality of life. He was still on many medications, including the chemotherapy pills, which many pancreatic cancer patients have to take indefinitely. He was also on antidepressants. One day he said, "Sweetheart, sometimes it takes everything in me not to pour them all down the drain." As I looked into his sad eyes I thought, *How does this glorify God? How does my father's needless suffering factor into any sort of divine plan?* This haunted my thoughts and made me incredibly angry. The worst part was that I couldn't say any of this to anyone—certainly not to my parents or my aunt Sandi. I couldn't say it to people at church either for fear of what my fellow congregants would think of me. I couldn't even bring myself to tell these thoughts to Russell, who had brought me to church in the first place. Once again I found myself putting on a cheerful face in front of others, only to cave into my fear and doubt when I was alone.

By July 2011, Mom and I were concerned that Dad was not gaining the weight back. She tried everything: cooking all his favorites dishes and hoping that he would enjoy them with the same gusto he had for the past forty years. It never happened. His appetite was fleeting at best, and every meal became a struggle for him to force something down. I tried not to think about the possible reasons for this and focused instead on the upcoming CAT scan of Dad's abdomen that Dr. Marks had ordered.

It is difficult to say why pancreatic cancer has such a high rate of recurrence. We do know that for many people it can return anywhere from a few months to a number of years after the original surgery. Sometimes it recurs in the pancreas, but often the cells from the original tumor are carried through the bloodstream to form so-called secondary tumors in the liver, lungs, lymph nodes, or any other number of organs. It is then referred to as metastatic pancreatic cancer and is as difficult to treat, if not more so, than the original disease. Often patients are feeling ill long before the recurrence is detected with a PET scan, CAT scan, or even blood tests, and they live in an awful limbo of fear and panic as they wait to learn their fate.

Somehow during the months when my father was cancer-free, three of these secondary tumors had grown in his liver; another was blocking his common bile duct. He also had fluid in his lungs. When Mom called on July 16 to give me the news, I didn't cry as I had the year before when she called me with the original diagnosis. I didn't go into shock either, because it was nothing less than I had expected all along. Somewhere inside I felt a little less guilty for doubting God and a little more justified for being angry with Him.

Dad's oncologist, Dr. Ferguson, was out of town when the results came in, so Dr. Marks informed Dr. Heslin, the surgeon who had performed the Whipple procedure several months earlier. Dr. Marks made an appointment for us to see Dr. Heslin. Dad was terribly ill that day, and as we stood in the waiting room of the Kirklin Clinic, Mom and I held him to try to stop his visible shaking from the fever. When Dr. Heslin's nurse came out to speak with us about the blood work, she didn't seem terribly concerned by Dad's condition; in fact it was clear from her impassive gaze and matter-of-fact tone that she had written him off already. I wanted to tell her that you don't speak to patients and their families this way, as if you're reading a grocery list. I wanted to tell her that the terminally ill and their families need compassion more than anyone else. I wanted to say a lot of things, but I couldn't bear to upset my parents further, and so I bit my tongue.

That was on a Friday. Over the weekend my father's condition steadily worsened, and by Sunday his temperature had risen to a dangerously high 103.1. When I called the hospital they said to bring him in immediately, but my father begged us not to. I stared at him: my once strong, proud father was now emaciated and pitifully ill. In that moment I felt my world shift in a truly ugly way. I had become the parent and he the child, and it was a feeling I wouldn't wish on anyone. Finally Mom and I gave in, deciding to hold off on the hospital for the time being.

By Monday morning, however, it was clear what we had to do; my father was getting sicker by the minute and if we didn't get him to the hospital he was going to die. Dad knew it, too, and he said he'd go, but only if he could ride in my car. I was relieved that he had stopped putting up a fight. But now we had another problem: he was too weak to get to the car, and my mother and I couldn't get him in safely and comfortably—not without help. In the end Russell called the sheriff's office, and they sent one of his fellow officers to my parents' house. That sweet man waited outside for thirty minutes; when we were ready, he climbed out of his cruiser and gently assisted Dad to my car.

After my father was admitted, Dr. Heslin determined that, like many pancreatic cancer patients, he needed surgery to open the common bile duct. This fairly simple procedure involves placing a stent, or tube, in the duct to keep the bile flowing properly. The problem was Dad's blood was so thin—a result of the tumors in his liver—that the doctor feared he would bleed to death on the operating table. We decided to wait until Wednesday—for surely his condition would stabilize by then. I listened to what Dr. Heslin had to say and nodded my agreement; then as discreetly as possible, I slipped out into the hall and cried hysterically. A few minutes later, I saw a hand reaching out to me, holding a tissue. It was Dr. Heslin.

"How much longer will I have my father?" I asked when I got the sobbing under control.

He told me that, assuming my father survived the procedure, he would probably live about three or four more months.

Monday and Tuesday dragged on, as we waited hour after hour for him to improve and prayed he didn't worsen.

He seemed to be stable enough on Tuesday evening, so I left for home, telling Mom to call me if his condition changed. She nodded, too exhausted to do anything else. I hugged her and walked out of the hospital. Like my mother I was also running on empty, and when I arrived at my house, nearly numb with fatigue, I found the thought of tossing and turning through another night unbearable. I know now that I wasn't thinking clearly when I took the Ambien, but it doesn't make me feel any less guilty. I downed the pill with a glass of water, slipped into bed, and fell into a deep, dreamless sleep.

I awoke at six o'clock the next morning, and as had become my habit over the past year, immediately looked at my cell phone. When I saw three missed calls from my mother, my body went into full panic mode. As I listened to Mom's frantic voice mails, I don't think my heart beat one time. My father had become

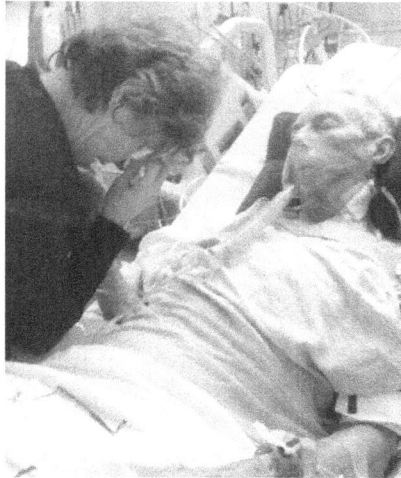

Fear, exhaustion, and grief taking over my mother as my father fought for his life.

septic, and they didn't think he would make it through the night.

I jumped out of bed and raced to the hospital, wracked with guilt for having taken the Ambien. If my father had died while I was sleeping, I didn't know how I would go on living. I don't think I took a full breath until I reached his room, held his hand, and felt the slow, stubborn beat of his pulse. I wept with gratitude, but it did nothing to dislodge the new brand of guilt sitting on my chest. My phone starting ringing, and when I saw it was Dr. Heslin, I stepped into the hallway to answer.

"It's time to make a tough decision, Dena," he said.

He was calling to tell me he wanted to do the procedure that morning, despite the enormous risk associated with it. If anything Dad's condition was worse than when we brought him in, and there was a very good chance he would die on the operating table. On the other hand, without the common bile duct stent he would surely die. Basically we had to make a decision now or never.

"Dena," Dr. Heslin said gently, "you need to tell me how heroic you want me to be today."

I knew he was asking about the lengths he should take to save my father's life and (his implication was) prolong my father's suffering. I also knew this call was a courtesy, because I was a fellow member of the tight-knit medical community. My exact words escape my memory, but I know I asked Dr. Heslin to please do whatever he could to save my dad.

Later that morning after they had once again taken my sweet dad to surgery, I was free to perform my next task: calling Aunt Sandi and my parents' friends David and Maureen to update them on his condition. I dreaded it, but at least it took my mind off my failings and gave me a sense of purpose.

Dr. Heslin was indeed a hero that day. The procedure was successful, and we all breathed a little easier—at least for the time being. Around noon Russell came to the hospital to have lunch with me. As we sat across the table from each other, I noticed my husband was acting strangely. He wasn't saying much, and he wasn't looking me in the eye. He just seemed off. When he left as soon as we finished eating, mumbling about getting back to work, I was shocked. It was completely unlike Russell to rush out without even seeing my dad. I had so many other things on my mind, though, that I didn't give it much thought. I went back to the room, pulled up a chair, and watched my father silently fight for his life.

When my cell phone rang later that afternoon, I wasn't concerned. After all I was there with my parents; there was no sudden seizing of my heart or cramping of my stomach, as there was when I thought someone might be calling with bad news about Dad. Imagine my shock when I heard a voice on the other end, telling me that Russell needed to go to the hospital. He had pulled his car over to the side of the road, because the pain in his head was so bad that his vision was blurred.

I ran out of the hospital and to my car, unsure of my own ability to drive. It was hard not to race there at ninety miles an hour, but I willed myself to stay just inside the speed limit, afraid of losing control of both the car and myself. When I got to Russell, he had his head in his hands and was pressing an ice pack to one temple. I helped him into my car and drove him not to the hospital where my father was but to Brookwood Medical Center where I work. It was closer. They immediately ushered him in for tests and me into a private waiting room where I sat paralyzed with fear as I waited to hear his fate. In my distraught state, I was convinced that not only was my father dying, but my husband was dying as well. I felt as though God was breaking me down, but I had no idea what His purpose was. I also didn't know how much more I could handle.

Why are You doing this to me? I asked Him bitterly. *How does this glorify You?*

I was no closer to an answer when, hours later, the doctor came out and told me that Russell wasn't dying; he

was suffering from a wicked migraine. He was given medi-
cation and discharged. I could take him home.

It was about 2:00 a.m. when we finally left the hospital,
and except for a snack that a kindly CRNA had brought
me hours earlier, I hadn't eaten since lunch. Between the
hunger, the stress, and the exhaustion, I honestly don't
know how my legs carried me to the car. I was still doing
better than my husband, however. He was so doped up
that he began walking to the car sideways! If it hadn't been
such a horrible day, I might have laughed at the sight of my
husband, a law enforcement officer and all-around straight
arrow, staggering through the parking lot like a drunken
sailor.

It's funny how some prayers are answered before we can
even utter them. That night I remember wishing for something delicious to eat, something I didn't have to cook. Fat
chance, right? Yet we walked into the house to find Tiffany,
our babysitter and saint-in-training, had ordered us a pizza.
We both fell upon it ravenously, and it was as if some part
of me was watching us from across the room and laughing.
We must have looked like two teenagers binge eating after a
night of binge drinking.

As Russell picked up his third slice, it suddenly dawned
on me what had happened. For months Russell had been
burning the candle at both ends. He was playing the role of

mother and father to Brooks and Willa, barely sleeping, and consuming a diet of sugary convenience. No wonder he had gotten his first—and since then only—migraine. I had been so busy taking care of my parents that I hadn't even noticed. I didn't think it was possible to feel guiltier, but there it was. I thanked God that my husband was okay, and I thanked Him for reminding me that miracles do still exist.

When I returned to the hospital the next day, I learned of another miracle. After getting the call about Dad the day before, David and Maureen (the same couple who had introduced Edna and Eddie all those years before) had driven three hours to be with my parents. They prayed over my dad, then left, as they had to get back home for work. Aunt Sandi came as well, making the long drive from Georgia to be with her brother. I was so grateful that, while I was at Brookwood with Russell, my parents were still surrounded by loving family and friends.

Grace also appeared in the form of Pastor Rick, who came to the hospital that Wednesday to speak to my father. When the pastor asked him if he had the Lord in his heart, Dad could barely answer. But even though his eyes were dazed and he was almost too weak to form words, he managed to say that he believed heaven is a beautiful place and that he would be there with the Lord when he passed. Rick was ministering directly to my sweet dad's soul, and this brought me a sort of peace I have scarcely known in my life. So many times I had wanted to ask Dad if he accepted Christ as his Lord and Savior, but I was petrified he would think I had given up on him. I left the hospital that night comforted by the knowledge that my father was not only an incredible person but a true Christian as well.

The rest of the week was a blur. Each day ran into the next and had the same dismal routine: get up, go to the hospital, help my parents until I could barely stand, go home, and stumble into bed, usually after a bout of hysterical crying. Some nights I poured myself a glass of wine, thinking it might calm me. It didn't but at least it knocked me out for a few precious hours until it all started again the next day. I barely saw Russell and the kids, and when I did I felt like only a part of me was there; the other part was sitting in a hospital room, watching over my dad, willing him to get well. Looking back, I don't know how I did it. I've gone over those days a million times in my mind, and the only answer is that every ounce of physical or mental strength came directly from God. Even in this terrible time, He was always there, supporting me and waiting for me to realize He had never left my side.

By the end of the week, Dr. Heslin determined that Dad was strong enough to undergo surgery the following Friday. The doctor believed a tumor was blocking his stomach and

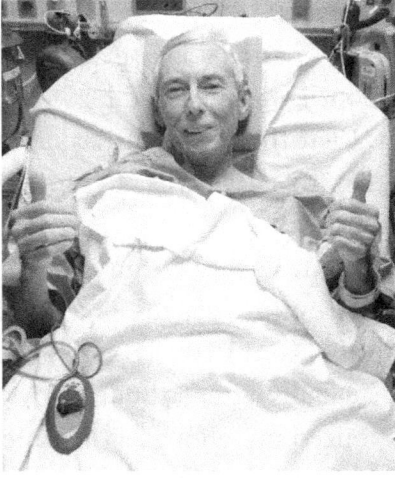

Ten days before Dad died, he was being wheeled into what would be his last surgery.

was the most likely reason for his lack of appetite. The plan was to insert a percutaneous endoscopic gastrostomy (PEG) tube to bypass the tumor until we could come up with our next plan of action. Once again Mom, Aunt Sandi, and I braced ourselves for a painful day of waiting, and once again we were amazed at my father's strength or at least his ability to fake it for our benefit. As the medical staff prepared to wheel him to the operating room, he smiled broadly and gave us two thumbs up. He held the pose just long enough for me to snap a picture; then they took him away.

It never gets easier to wait for someone you love to get out of surgery. With your stomach in knots, you try to imagine what's happening in the operating room. You will the doctor to make the right decisions; you imagine you can steady his hands as he cuts into your loved one's heart, lungs, kidney, or abdomen. If you're like me, you hope for these things, and if you're like me, you know it's not in your hands or the doctor's hands. It's in God's hands, and not knowing what He has decided is an agony. You wait for the doctor to emerge so you can gauge his expression; you pray to hear the words "your dad/mom/sister/brother/husband/child has survived."

About an hour later, a nurse came to tell us that my father had indeed survived, and we could see him as soon as he left the recovery room. As Mom, Sandi, and I headed to the conference room to meet with Dr. Heslin, I heard Mom or Aunt Sandi sigh with relief and I shuddered. They thought this was good news; I knew the surgery should have been much longer.

Where there's life, there's hope, I reminded myself.

I had been praying so hard for Dad to make it through the operation that I was quite unprepared for what might come next. We were barely settled in our seats when Dr. Heslin entered the room, his face carefully neutral. Mom and Aunt Sandi wore grateful smiles, but I felt my stomach drop, because I knew that expression only too well. Sure enough the doctor pulled out his pad and pencil, just as he had done the year before to show us where Dad's original tumor was. But this time he didn't just sketch the now-familiar shape of the pancreas; he included several other abdominal organs as well. We silently waited for him to finish, and just when the sound of the pencil scratching across the page became unbearable, he stopped drawing and looked up at us.

"I'm afraid the cancer has spread even more than we thought," he said, pointing to the sketch. "As the scan showed, it's in his liver, but it's also showered all over his peritoneum, stomach, and intestines."

He went on to say that when they opened him up and saw how extensive it was, they just inserted the PEG tube and closed him up again. Suddenly I felt as though I was being lifted out of my body and was hovering above the room. It was the same surreal feeling I'd had when Dad was first diagnosed. I saw Mom and Aunt Sandi's mouths moving, but their voices sounded like they were miles away. With eyes wide and almost childlike, they were asking about a new treatment plan. Was another surgery possible? How soon could my father start IV chemotherapy? Was radiation a viable option this time?

There are indeed treatments for a recurrence of pancreatic cancer; I knew this, because I had done the research just in case. Like the treatments following an original diagnosis, they include more chemotherapy. They may be the same drugs that were administered the first time around, or they may be completely different. Some patients opt for experimental drugs as part of a clinical trial. Although the side effects vary from person to person, they tend to be as brutal, if not worse than the earlier treatment. Surgery is also sometimes an option, but this depends on how far the cancer has spread and to which organs it has spread.

I scanned their faces, taking in the irrationally hopeful expressions of my mom and aunt as well as the grim, straight line of Dr. Heslin's mouth. That's when the thought ran through my mind and took root. I didn't know if I was being cold hearted or simply realistic, but I knew I had to say it for my father's sake. I was reminded of that day, so long ago, when he had refused to let me come home from college. It had killed him to say the words, killed him to hear me crying and pleading to him about how lonely and miserable I was. I heard his voice then, the voice of my sweet dad before cancer had stolen his confidence: "It was the hardest thing I ever had to do, Sweetheart, but it was best for you."

Suddenly I knew what I had to say. The question was how to get the words past the lump in my throat. The answer again was God. From somewhere deep inside me, He gave me the strength to say the unthinkable.

"When do we just stop?"

My voice was low and fragile, like it might break into a thousand pieces. Then the lump expanded in my throat, and I couldn't say anything else. Mom and Aunt Sandi's heads whipped around to face me, and I couldn't tell if they were angry or merely confused by the question. Dr. Heslin, though, didn't move. I saw just the slightest flicker in his gaze, and I was once again struck by the awful position he was in. No matter how brilliant a surgeon he was, no matter how strong his intention to heal, he would always have to deliver news that shattered lives in an instant. My mother turned to him, pleading, but he kept his gaze steady on mine.

"Right now," he said, calmly and softly but assertively.

I thought I detected a fleeting look of relief on his face.

"We stop all this right now."

As soon as he spoke, I felt my body go limp (my own version of relief). I had known the answer to the question before I asked it, but I needed him to say it. I couldn't bear the thought of anyone—Mom, Aunt Sandi, and especially my dad—thinking I had given up on him. My mother seemed shocked by Dr. Heslin's response, and for a moment I thought she might actually faint. Then she slowly nodded.

"W-well…." She paused for a moment, trying to collect herself. "Where do we go from here?"

Dr. Heslin glanced to me as if he were asking for support; then he turned back to my mother.

"The priority now," he said gently, "is to make Eddie as comfortable as possible."

We all knew what that meant: now we had to find a way to tell my father. We had never kept anything about his condition from him, and we weren't about to start. Given his mental state over the past several months, I had no idea how badly he would take the news, but to my surprise he wanted to fight. He wanted chemo; he wanted to get well. With a heavy heart, I promised him that as soon as he was strong enough he could begin treatment. It wasn't a lie exactly; I just knew it was never going to come to that.

We spent the next few days waiting for Dad to be well enough to go home, which would now be on hospice. The perversity of this escaped no one. When they released him on Tuesday morning, Dad, once again, begged to ride in my car, but knowing that wasn't possible, I went straight to the house to make sure everything was ready for his arrival. Russell and a friend had already rearranged the furniture to accommodate a hospital bed in my parents' room, and as I walked through the once-familiar rooms, I was shocked to find them so changed. Sighing, I went to wait on the front steps. I was glad my parents would have at least a few precious moments alone.

Finally I saw the ambulance coming up the street; a few cars trailed behind it, reminding me of a funeral procession. As it pulled up in front of my parents' house, I stood and pulled my phone from my pocket. My father would never again leave his home alive, and I felt compelled to document his journey. I snapped pictures of the ambulance and of the EMTs helping the emaciated, nearly unrecognizable figure inside. My dad wanted to go straight to his recliner, and as I watched the paramedics gently settling him in, I stopped asking God for a miracle and began praying for his peace and comfort.

It was the last time we had any control over the house. After that it was a flurry of hospice nurses and friends bringing food, prayers, and comfort. My parents' neighbor Joey came over to help my father, first from the recliner to the wheelchair, then from the wheelchair to the bed. I made sure to walk each guest to the door when he or she left. My dad had always insisted on this bit of civility when I was growing up, and it made me proud to honor him in this way and to keep this one thing normal for him.

Aunt Sandi, who had returned home to Georgia after my dad's last surgery, now went to Florida to get my grand-father, and they, too, came to stay at my parents' house. I resumed a nearly round-the-clock schedule of taking care of my husband and children and helping my parents. On a daily basis, I fought the anger and sorrow that constantly threatened to bubble to the surface. My father, who had never done anything but good, would eventually succumb to the terrible disease gnawing away at his body. My mother, instead of enjoying her golden years with her life partner, would be mourning him. I refused to let my emotions control me; instead I decided I would be her rock. I would bear as much of the burden as I could. In short I would step into my father's role as the family's caretaker, using the lessons he had taught me throughout my life.

"God, help me," I prayed each morning. "Please help me get through another day, to be strong for them as they have always been strong for me."

When I wasn't praying, I thought about all the encouraging e-mails my father had sent me while I was in college.

"You can do it, sweetheart," he often wrote, reminding me of the inner strength I had, if only I would learn to trust and rely on it.

One day I overheard a hospice nurse speaking with a colleague on the phone.

"Mr. Dixon won't be with us much longer," she said, unaware that I was standing behind her nearly hyperventilating with panic.

Sure, I acted strong around everyone—no one needed my tears. But there were often days when I felt like I was losing my mind, especially when the everyday demands of being a wife and mother piled on top of my nightmarish existence. One day when Dad was still in the hospital, my mother asked me to go to the house and pick up some clothes for him. On my way I stopped to pick up Brooks and Willa from school; then I stopped at the vet to get our dog CJ. I got everyone situated in the back of the car and headed over to my parents' house. I was so lost in my own thoughts that I wasn't paying much attention to what was going on in the back seat. Suddenly I heard Brooks yell, "Oh, no, Mama! CJ done throwed up all over me!"

One glance in the rearview mirror revealed that the dog had indeed vomited all over my son. I told everyone to stay put until we got to Mae Mae's (my kids' nickname for my mother). It seemed to take forever, but I finally pulled into my parents' driveway, threw the car in park, and hopped out to get a wet towel, so I could clean up the mess. I had no sooner closed the door behind me when CJ jumped out of Brooks' lap and, with a well-placed paw, locked the car door. Brooks, Willa, CJ and her vomit, and my cell phone were inside. It was a brutally hot July day in Alabama, and I thanked God the car was running and the air conditioner was on. The chaotic scene was something Russell and I normally would laugh about over dinner; that day when I was in a rush to get back to my parents, it almost did me in. On days like this, that strength my father mentioned was nowhere to be found.

Even with the incredible hospice staff, caring for Dad was a round-the-clock job. By this point he was so weak he couldn't even walk from the bed to the bathroom. As badly as I wanted to help with everything, I hung back and let my mother handle these private moments. It was agonizing to watch them slowly shuffle down the hall to the bathroom—my father's rail-thin frame leaning on my mother's arm for support. As horrified as I was by his condition, I couldn't begin to imagine how my mother felt as her husband of four decades and the father of her children wasted away before her eyes.

Mom was working herself to the bone, preparing my father's food, giving him his meds, sitting up with him when he was in pain. As I watched her wear a path between the bedroom, the kitchen, and the bathroom, I began to fear for her mental and physical health. I went to my parents' house whenever I could, but she insisted on doing the bulk of the work herself. It was only when she began to sway and her eyes took on that vacant, glassy look that I was able to persuade her to go to bed. She rarely was able to sleep, though, and when she did it was only because her exhausted body gave her absolutely no other choice. That's when I took over, keeping an eye on my father and often having to help him use the bathroom or take a shower. His humiliation at having his daughter care for him in this way was unbearable to me, so I tried to talk to him about other things: what Russell was up to, how things were going at work, something funny that Brooks or Willa had done. It was the first time in my life that we avoided telling each other what was really on our minds. Now I communicated my love and respect for him by bringing him his meals and meds and easing him back into bed after the short but draining walks around the house. I could tell by the way he looked at me that Dad understood what I was going through. He understood that it was breaking my heart to see him in this way and that I was afraid of losing him. Even as he faced the end of his life, he felt sorry for me, and I was incredibly humbled by his selflessness. It was one of those rare times during his illness when I was able to step out of my pain and see the beauty of the experience; it was in those moments that I felt God's grace upon my family and me.

My aunt Sandi was another godsend. She and my father had gone through a rough period in their relationship, which ended when Sandi was diagnosed with breast cancer many years before. She had beaten it, thank God, and since then they had never been closer. Now she insisted on feeding him his last meals, and my mother selflessly let her have the experience. The love that passed silently between brother and sister each time she held the spoon to his lips was one of the most amazing things I have ever seen.

"Cancer reunited us," she said one day, choking back tears, "and now it's tearing us apart again."

Even with all of us helping, though, things got missed. We noticed Dad was feeling more and more nauseous with each passing day. Imagine our horror when it dawned on us that his PEG tube needed to be drained. My mother immediately connected his gastric tube to gravity, and within minutes it had drained over 500 ccs of fluid. As I watched my dad sigh in relief, I felt a lead ball in my own stomach, a hard knot of guilt. Imagine me, a nurse, and I didn't think of the tube! When I glanced at Mom, I knew she felt the same way. Looking back, I can see it was not so much guilt we were feeling but a complete and utter helplessness. It was also the beginning of my realization that none of us—ill or not—is in control of our lives. Everything, except our love for and reliance on God, is an illusion, and a painful one to let go of.

Despite everything we did, Dad's condition slowly deteriorated. Each day I took his blood pressure, and each day it was a bit lower. Cancer was stealing his life bit by agonizing bit. Then on the Monday after he came home, things suddenly took a rapid turn for the worse. I had decided to take my grandfather to dinner, just to get him out of the house for a while. We were only gone about two hours, but when we returned my father seemed drastically changed. As I looked down at him, struggling to breathe, I knew it wouldn't be long. It suddenly hit me how unprepared I was for this, and I turned to Aunt Sandi in a panic.

"What am I going to do?"

Through the fog I heard the pleading sound in my voice and knew that I had, once again, become the child. Aunt Sandi just looked at me for a moment, as if gauging what to say.

"You go get a pair of your dad's pajama pants and put them on. Then you call your husband and tell him you're not coming home tonight."

"Yes, ma'am," I replied, incredibly grateful that someone else was calling the shots.

I had said countless prayers over the past year, but none of these prayers were more fervent than to be present when my father took his last breath. The very thought that I might be home or asleep when he left this world was intolerable. That Monday night we pushed the beds together in my parents' room so that Mom, Dad, and I could be as close to each other as possible. Utterly exhausted, I was asleep within in minutes.

At 4:21 a.m. the Lord woke me up. I know it was Him, because I jumped up from a sound, dreamless sleep and pulled myself into a sitting position. I looked over at my father and watched his chest slowly rise and fall. I stayed that way for the next nine minutes, and at exactly 4:30 I gently woke up my mom.

"I think it's time, Mom."

Mom turned to her beloved and gently placed her hand

on his chest. My father took one more ragged breath and slipped silently away. Almost immediately my mother got up, pulled on her clothes, and went to wake the others. I stayed in bed, listening to everyone rush around, trying to ward off the flood of pain that awaited them. My own numbness ended when my eighty-nine-year-old grandfather shuffled into the room and headed for the hospital bed. His face crumpling, he reached for his son's hand and began to sob.

It was finally over.

CHAPTER V

The Aftermath of the Storm

"Three different times I begged the Lord to take [my pain] away. Each time He said, 'My gracious favor is all you need. My power works best in your weakness.' So now I am glad to boast about my weaknesses, so that the power of Christ may work through me. Since I know it is all for Christ's good, I am quite content with my weaknesses and with insults, hardships, persecutions, and calamities. For when I am weak then I am strong."
—2 Corinthians 12:8-10 (New Living Translation Bible)

As I wrote this last chapter, my father's death hurt just as much, if not more, than the day it happened a little over a year before. The purpose of this book was never to tell people that with God the pain disappears; it hasn't been true for me, and even if it were, I would never proclaim it was the truth for another. My purpose in writing this is to help others understand that God not only brings you through the painful times, He also uses them to deliver His grace.

Oftentimes God delivers grace through other people. When Pastor Rick ministered to my father in the hospital, I thought it was to make sure he was going to heaven. I now know that Dad's soul was never in jeopardy; the real purpose of that conversation was to let me know I would see him again.

God also used our fellow church congregants to bring us comfort. Some brought hot meals to my house, so I didn't have to worry about cooking for Russell and the kids. Others knew my mother faced a mountain of medical bills and left envelopes of money, despite the fact that they had never even met my parents.

I was also blessed with the loving support of my coworkers. On the Sunday before Dad died, Trish, my friend and colleague, called to see how he was doing. I was scheduled to work that night, but when Trish heard my voice (I kept repeating, "I don't know, I don't know"), she ordered me to stay put. She took my shift, cutting short her own vacation to do so.

But one of the most precious gifts God has ever given me was the night I got to spend alone with my father. We had always spoken about anything and everything, and I had sorely missed these heart-to-hearts over the past year. Either he was going to the doctor, or I was going to work. Often I just didn't want to burden him with my problems. More recently he was just too sick. But in that week before he died, he had one particularly lucid night. I sat by his bed and held his hand, rubbing my thumb along the thin, dry skin. We talked about so many important things that night, including my dad's love for Russell and his approval of him as a husband and father. He told me how proud he was of me as a wife, mother, and nurse anesthetist, as well as a daughter. Even in Dad's darkest hour, he validated every significant life choice I had made. I was also able to put his mind at ease by promising to take care of my mother after he was gone.

Another blessing came after he had passed away. Not wanting my mother to pack up Dad's possessions alone, I went over to help. She told me to take anything as a keepsake, but there was only one thing I wanted: the silver coin I had given him on my wedding day. I tore the house apart that afternoon but couldn't find it anywhere. Had he lost it? There was no way he'd get rid of it on purpose.

Oh, this is silly, I thought. *It's just a cheap little thing.*

It wasn't until sometime later that the mystery was solved. Mom was at the bank, going through Dad's safety deposit box. As she reached in to grab a stack of legal documents, a flash of silver caught her eye. As soon as her hand closed around it, she knew what it was. Mom called immediately to tell me the news, and when I heard the smile in her voice, I started crying. They were tears of both joy and sadness, but I didn't know which was harder to bear.

Through my father's illness and death, God also taught me to reassess my priorities. My life has always been about unending obligations (isn't everyone's?), but before my dad got sick, I was confused about what my true responsibilities were. I thought I had to be the perfect wife, mother, daughter, and nurse. I thought I had to be the perfect Christian—whatever that means. The moment my dad died, I let go of everything and God took over. He was my life support and my ventilator; I know this because there was no way I would have been able to breathe under the crushing weight of my grief. If I had acted according to my earthly heart, I never would have survived the heartache, fear, and terror of losing my dad. I didn't realize it at the time, but I got through it by leaning on God's power, comfort, and love.

The very wise Dean Marian Baur of Samford University once said, "Dena, the world doesn't care how you feel. They only care what you believe." I knew at the time that her words were profound, but I only truly understood after my dad died. I believe that Jesus is the Christ and the Son of the living God. He is my Lord and Savior.

This new confidence in my beliefs has affected every aspect of my life, including my work. I now ask my patients if I could pray with and for them. I also touch them more, often rubbing their foreheads as I put them under anesthesia. Just as my sweet children want me to "kiss it" when they are hurting, my sweet patients crave comfort and compassion before surgery.

More than ever I want to be all God made me to be, but I understand this is an evolutionary process that will continue throughout my life. As it says in Hebrews 11:1, "Now faith is being sure of what we hope for and certain of what we do not see." Having obedient faith will never make earthly sense. Each time I am at church, I am reminded not only of the material things I have been blessed with but also of how little those things matter. The moment my dad drew his last breath, his possessions meant nothing. All that mattered was the loving father, husband, son, brother, and friend he had been, and this knowledge has made me re-evaluate my own place in the world. Worldly acceptance no longer means much to me, and gossip, once so enjoyable, is not as juicy—in fact it just makes me sad.

I am trying everyday to live in the *freedom* of enough. I am enough for me, and I am enough for God. I now know that when I leave this world, it won't matter how thin, rich, or popular I was. The only things that matter will be:

- What kind of wife was I?
- What kind of mother was I?
- What kind of friend was I?
- How did I treat my coworkers?

- How did I touch the lives of my patients?
- How did I treat my neighbors?
- How did I handle difficult situations?
- What did I do for God's kingdom?
- How did I impact or influence the lives of everyone I touched? Did I pray with or for them?

I have learned the best—and hardest—lessons of my life through my failures. My dad taught me that, but God taught me that I can't walk with Jesus if, at some point in my life, I haven't been broken. I've also learned through my talents as well, and I no longer apologize for being competitive, striving for excellence, or refusing to quit. I know now that it's okay to start your faith in God with a crisis in your life; it's just not okay to stay in that crisis. You have to trust in the Lord and then wait on the confirmation of what He will do.

I was at church recently singing in the audience where only I could hear myself (not up front—I can't carry a tune at all). The song's chorus was "I'll stand with arms high and heart abandoned in awe of the one who gave it all."

Suddenly I felt my arms raising, as if of their own volition. I had never done that before, and I knew it meant I was letting go. I finally felt free to admit to anyone around me that I believe in myself and my relationship with the Lord. I began to cry, but for the first time in a long time, they were tears of joy. For in that moment, my tears and upturned hands were my most passionate prayers.

And God knew.

The Eulogy I Read
at My Father's Funeral

In June 2010 I made a phone call to my dear friend Amanda. I told her I had something to get off of my chest and she was the only friend in my life I thought would not think I was crazy for what I was about to say. I told her I had no idea what it was, but God was preparing me for something big—something I was not going to like. I said it out loud to a trusting soul, and I felt better.

About a month later, my sweet dad was diagnosed with cancer. I remember calling Russell sobbing, and then Amanda. It still had not clicked in my head that maybe this was the "something bad." Long story short, Dad had surgery, received treatments, felt sick, felt better, felt sick, and felt better, and through it all I realized his cancer wasn't the something for which God was preparing me. Standing here talking to you was what God was preparing me to do. You see, I am a woman of faith. I fear the Lord, I love the Lord, but I do not have the self-confidence to teach you about Him and His word. I never have. In fact, I have never prayed aloud in a small group, at church, or even with my loving husband over our meals.

Many things unfolded in my mind after my dad became ill. In times like these you begin to reminisce and think about the past. I remembered I'd had many, many printed e-mails from my dad. You see when I was in college, Dad would write me a quick note before he went to work every morning. Some reflected a great day, some rainy-day blues, some anger, and so on. He just wrote to me about life, about what he was going through that day, and most important of all every e-mail had words of encouragement. While I was away at college, all he desired was to see me succeed, to graduate. As I read through the e-mails, I realized Dad had written his own euology without even knowing it.

These are quotes taken directly from his e-mails:

- Keep your chin up, your ambitions high, and be selective in your road in life.

- You can and will be whatever you set your mind on.
- Depending on someone else is okay if that someone is the right one.
- Dedication is worth whatever it takes to be successful.
- I am where I am in life because I choose to be.
- Set your goals in the quantum range.
- Set goals that are not just acceptable but beyond comprehension.
- Don't let the challenges in life get in the way of being all you can be.
- Do not accept everything you are taught; challenge what you do not understand, and learn to think openly.
- We have the opportunity to accept His offering to be saved or sit on our duffs and let this wonderful offering go unattended.
- Reach out and grasp life with zeal and enthusiasm, and make your future what you want it to be.
- Mom and I cannot and will not be the reason for your failure or success. That is up to you.
- Money gets in the way of happiness.
- If it is worth working for then it's certainly worth having.

- If it weren't for dads like me, girls like Mom and you would be broke, homeless, and looking for love. By the way, don't let Mom see this, because she won't agree and she would cut me off.
- We just need to sit back and appreciate who we are, where we are, and look at what we have to be proud of.
- What you do is what you get.
- Don't let the little downs between those great highs be anything other than stepping-stones to your success.
- Be all you can be, and stay out of the Army.
- Watch your rear end—it will change shape in a hurry.
- You must always be a caring and understanding person, aware of others and their feelings.
- If you just sit back and become the rug on the floor, then expect to be walked on, cleaned occasionally, and always expected to be there in good condition for the next step.
- You will receive what you deserve for the efforts you make.

- God did not promise us an easy time in life; He just promised us a good life.
- Releases of frustrations are life-saving actions, so if you need to, yell like hell!
- If you ask for guidance in your prayers, you will get answers.
- Being first or the best is not always the happiest rule in life.
- Always respect yourself and others with truth, honesty, and integrity and you will be successful in every endeavor.
- Many times we have failed to understand the changes that have taken place in our lives; however we accept those changes and go on to have wonderfully fulfilled lives.
- We often forget that all things are created and planned before we are ready for them.
- Our future is planned, and the plan maker is greater than we can imagine.
- Opportunities are before you every day of your life; what you choose to do with them will determine your success.
- Today is the beginning of a new view of an old horizon.

- As always, your wonderful, loving, not so rich,
  but happy father.

In these sad times, many family members and friends ask, "What can we do for you?" and say, "Call if you need anything." And normally families say "thank you," and that we will. That is not what I am going to say to you today. I need to know that my father's death was used by God to help bring others closer to Him. My father loved the Lord, and he wants to know that you love Him too. So here is what you can do for our family—for my mom, my brother, my aunt, my papa: go to church on Sunday. God says a church is a place where two or more are gathered together in His name. So choose your church, and if you have already accepted Jesus Christ as your lord and savior then lift my family in prayers, for over the next few days, weeks, month, and years there will be difficult times, and we will need that support. If you haven't asked Jesus Christ to be your lord and savior, the one and only path to eternal life, then please just take a moment and repeat the words just as my dad did. It is something so simple. Believe it in your heart and confess it with your mouth that Jesus Christ is the son of the living God, and only through Him you will achieve eternal life.

Thank you for loving my family and for being here to celebrate such an amazing life that made a positive impact on so many. Go home today and hold your loved ones tightly and thank our creator for them. None of us are without our shortcomings (I sure know I have mine), but none of us are without love.

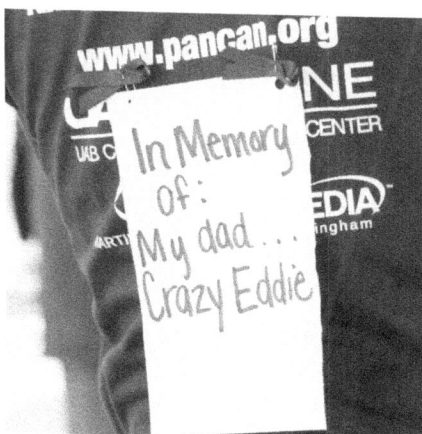

For more information on pancreatic cancer,
please visit www.pancan.org